THE THEORY OF NEED IN MARX

AGNES HELLER

The Theory of Need in Marx

ALLISON & BUSBY, LONDON
in association with Spokesman Books

First published in Great Britain by
Allison & Busby Limited, 6a Noel Street, London W1V 3RB
in association with
Spokesman Books, Bertrand Russell House, Gamble Street,
Nottingham.

ISBN 0 85031 168 3 hardback
ISBN 0 85031 174 8 paperback

Set in Lectura and printed by
Villiers Publications Ltd, Ingestre Road, London NW5 1UL

CONTENTS

INTRODUCTION

Theories of underconsumption, according to Keynes, hibernated until J. A. Hobson flung himself with unavailing ardour against the ranks of orthodoxy. The theory of *need* has been totally neglected in Keynes and all other economic orthodoxies. This is surprising because the world at large innocently believes that the whole purpose of economic activity, of production and distribution, is to satisfy human needs and that economists are those who make their special concern the ways and means of doing so. In the works of economists or the history of economic thought there are analyses — written at great length and with great complexity — of demand and supply, money, the market and market competition. But there is nothing about need (save some little noted work by Bastiat in the last century and by Professor Champernowne in this). The mainstream of academic economics has had nothing to say. The reason for this is that it is *assumed* right away at the outset that the market automatically indicates human needs. A much used text book of the thirties distinguished for its obsequious but lucid exposition of acceptable doctrine (Benham's *Economics*) writes:

"One intermediary buys from another in the hope that, after transforming the commodity into a form suitable for satisfying wants, he in turn will be able to sell it at a profit. The chain may be very long, but always at the end of it stands the final consumer who buys the consumers' goods. We conclude, therefore, that the rationale of economic activity is to satisfy human wants by producing consumers' goods."

This said, the whole question of wants and needs is, from the standpoint of economic theory, closed. The human being's needs are treated as a given factor, a sort of instinctive endowment; armed with this he or she enters the market place as buyer and seller to put in "unwanted" work (disutility) and take out "wanted" commodities (utility). If wants can be satisfied, the market will produce them; if they cannot, their non-availability on the market or non-purchasability will signal this fact. If, that is, the market is working properly. If it is not, then the economist is the expert who advises on how to repair it. So the whole of economic science becomes the study — in health and sickness — of these market mechanisms mediated by money.

This was also the arena for Karl Marx's economic studies, but there was an important difference. At the outset he suspected deep flaws in this commodity market system. True, it swept away the brutishness, cruelty and superstition of land ownership with serfdom, but, as he wrote in the early days when he was trying to think out the problems to which it was most necessary to orientate his research:

"We have seen what significance, given socialism, the *wealth* of human need has, and what significance, therefore, both a *new mode of production* and a new *object* of production have: a new manifestation of the forces of *human* nature and a new enrichment of *human* nature. Under private property their significance is reversed: every person speculates on creating a *new* need in another, so as to drive him to a fresh sacrifice, place him in a new dependance and to seduce him into a new mode of *gratification* and therefore economic ruin. Each tries to establish over the other an *alien power*, so as thereby to find satisfaction of his own selfish need. The increase in the quantity of objects is accompanied by an extension of the realm of the alien powers to which man is subjected, and every new product represents a new *possibility* of mutual swindling and mutual plundering. Man becomes ever poorer as man, his need for *money* becomes ever greater if he wants to overpower hostile beings. The power of his *money* declines so to say in inverse proportion to the increase in the volume of production: that is, his neediness grows as the *power* of money increases. The need for money is therefore the true need produced by the modern economic system, and it is the only need which the latter produces." (*Economic and Philosophic Manuscripts of 1844*, page 147, London, Lawrence and Wishart, 1970)

And later on Marx adds: "Money is the *pimp* between man's need and the object, between his life and his means of life" (page 165).

In a world still swearing by Adam Smith and free trade, critical analysis of this money system, this commodity or market system

8

was the crucial, essential means towards opening a way to a *new mode of production*. This critical analysis Marx made a life work —the *Grundrisse* and *Capital* — and it constituted an overwhelmingly powerful proof that the commodity-based structure of capitalism would have to be superseded by some new social structure if the needs of men and women *as human beings* are to be met. The commodity, money, capital, "the economy" — i.e. the whole development process of market relations which the academic economists *assume* must *automatically* reflect human needs — far from satisfying human needs, in fact makes this "devoutly to be wished" goal less and less attainable. True, all sorts of new powers and forces are released as the processes of the capital and money system unfold with the whole world as their arena; but these forces are out of control. The problem is to harness and control them. For all their horrors, we may well allow that these explosive new economic forces have galvanised new human activities and opened new potentialities, freeing human beings from the oppressive torpor of earlier societies. But now they threaten to destroy the species, maybe in a holocaust, maybe person by person, psychologically as much as physically.

The historical explosion of industrial capitalism can be nothing but a *transitional* process, raising at once the question: "After the commodity, money, market economy, what?" If an economy structured on commodity relations fails to meet the *really human* needs of human beings, what structure of social and economic relations can take its place? Out of our present mess where is it that we are trying to get? This is the really important question; not because we can leap all at once into some brave new world, but because we need to find a direction, however we move — step by step, inch by inch or mile by mile, as opportunities occur. Otherwise we just go on going round in circles. Marx's analysis and our present experiences of the socio-economic structure of capitalism demonstrate that its problems are not peripheral and correctable but are rooted in the structure itself. They become more and more acute as time goes on. If this failing structure is one based on the socio-economic relations of commodity exchange, to what new structural forms should we change and how? This question cannot be answered until we think far more deeply and see far more clearly what our real

9

needs as human beings are and recognise the forms of distortion and perversion to which the socio-economy of capitalism subjects our humanity. We talk glibly of socialism as "production for use"; this is meaningful as posing an antithesis to production for the market. A thing is useful because it meets a human need. Adam Smith taught that the market would inform the producer what he should produce. If the market is set aside or used only subordinately, who decides what is to be produced and how? What are the really human needs of really human activity?

The great value of Agnes Heller's work is that it opens the way to thinking far more deeply and far more clearly about human needs and the importance of this concept in the shaping of Marx's analysis. For in this respect Marx has been sorely misunderstood, not least by "marxists". The very scientific quality of his analysis of the contemporary phase of human society has been, as it were, turned against him in that people continue to follow him talking about what is and was, and they seem to have lost sensitivity to the fact that historical forces, the living activities and consciousness of people, are pressing hard against the "natural trends" of the market and commodity system. The time has come to be more concerned with the alternative — how to organise the essentials of social existence and human survival in such a way as to open better possibilities of satisfying, more directly and more simply, the real needs of thinking, imagining, active, loving human beings.

At the present time needs, obvious needs are not being met, and resources — people and plants — that might help to meet them, are idle. But, it is said, we are in an economic crisis; the prime need is to overcome this crisis, only then can further material needs be tackled, needs for better education, better health services, better transport, housing, education and so forth. To deal with the crisis, it is asserted, public expenditure must be cut. Well, say some, if that is so why not cut military expenditure? No, say others, defence is a need overriding all others; and so the argument goes on. But all this is not only a matter of argument; it is a matter of decision-taking and where the decisions are taken is, as a rule, some way distant from the public argument.

Underlying the resolution of these immediate problems is the structure of the social system in which they are resolved and the political and economic mechanisms for so doing. There are many questions here to which enough thought has not yet been given. What are needs? How do they arise? Who decides priorities in meeting them? Unemployment, frustration and isolation, hateful and meaningless work, pollution of the atmosphere, the squandering of scarce resources, the stresses and insecurity of modern life, the threat of unthinkable forms of war, the perverted use of advanced science, bureaucratic waste and absurd hierarchies of status and pay, all these ills of the present time are to be set against the undoubted advances in caring public consciousness, concern for the rights of the worker at work, recognition — though as yet not far reaching — that, in addition to wages and conditions of work, unions and other workers' organisations must concern themselves with the social use of labour. But the attempts to institutionalise these progressive aspirations in a "welfare state" hooked on to a capitalist market economy — the "mixed economy" — even where successful, are perilously insecure and constantly open to attack "to save the system from the threat of crisis". What is the "system" that is being saved? Are its needs compatible with "caring public consciousness" and the "needs" of democracy? How little thought has been put into the understanding of these basic questions by socialist economists and sociologists! And how closely these questions are related to problems of social change and effective action to achieve change.

Agnes Heller's work enables us to think about these problems from the standpoint of socialist theory and to look beyond the restricting structure of capitalism and its market economy. Too much political and economic argument today ends up within the preconceptions of an economic system which is actually *controlled* by the market and its money system, and which is unable itself to control the market and monetary forces that stultify all our efforts to meet the needs of *people* more effectively. The needs of capital, of profitable production, oust the needs of people. Adam Smith's apologia for the market system — valid enough in its day, two hundred years ago — argued that the market would automatically discover and meet people's needs. This, even in the past, was only true in a limited sense; but, far from the market system overcoming its defects, these are multiplied and amplified with the development of the system and the concentration of capital into increasingly huge units. The development

11

of the system declares very loudly the necessity of treating this socio-economic structure as transitory. This means seeking a deeper understanding of needs and looking for new ways of meeting them.

An important aspect of these problems emerges from the ecological debate which has rightly received a great deal of attention. The failure of the market mechanisms raises the whole problem of popular participation in social planning to a new level of urgency. The wisdom of allowing market forces to determine, unfettered, the rate of use of scarce natural resources is today being questioned with far greater insistence than was formerly the case. Entrepreneurs cite the market as their alibi for the systematic misuse of materials and also of people; but today more people come back at them saying "so much the worse for the market". However, even before this recent growth of concern about the market system's destruction of the human environment, demand for great extensions of democratic power was already becoming urgent.

During the post-war years state intervention in the administration of privately controlled economies has increased greatly. Concomitantly, publicly controlled enterprise and welfare provision of public services has also increased creating large sectors of advanced economies which could be made less subordinate to market pressures. This area of public control could serve to a certain extent as a counter-influence to the free operation of the market. It cannot be said that much has yet been achieved in this respect, since there is extraordinary confusion about the principles and objectives that should guide non-market enterprises. However this has resulted in a notable revival of concern with the concept of *need*, as distinct from the conventional economic notion of *demand*, which has dominated social thinking as long as the rationality of the market remained virtually unchallenged.

Of course the system based on market and monetary criteria is the only system that the higher echelons of the hierarchies of power are familiar with; it is also the social structure best adapted to the maintenance and support of their hierarchical status. They find it hard to think of alternatives and are hardly likely to encourage any exploration of alternatives. But the needs of people and the impact of developing democratic forces to

12

express these needs bring new pressures to bear on the market structure. The imagined sovereignty of "demand" is obviously linked with the hegemony or desired hegemony of the market over all socio-economic decisions. The conventional distinction between "effective" demand and its implied ghost, "non-effective" demand, which would be sheer nonsense within any strict interpretation of market-based economic models, reflects an uneasy (if usually incomplete) recognition of the human or social inadequacy of that model. It has long been generally recognised, for instance, that market forces alone will never meet the housing need, or the health need, of large sectors of the population working in even the most successful market economies.

The evolution of market capitalism has belied the more rosy hopes of Adam Smith and John Stuart Mill. Wealth is concentrated in huge multinational enterprises. Resources are badly allocated and income unequally distributed. Within the market's sway, larger or lesser groups of people lack the resources to translate some of their basic needs into "effective demand". Hence the growth of public provision and of watchful underdog pressure groups in all the major economies. Orthodox economists were not always blind to these difficulties, and Marshall, for instance, troubled himself with the distinction not only between "necessities" and other commodities, but also between the "necessities of efficiency" and the necessities of existence. But whilst all necessities were either provided in the market place or not at all, it remained an abstract preoccupation, and "need" was condemned to seem a phantom idea outside the writings of utopians and socialists.

Today, in the self-styled welfare states, the existence of a large infrastructure of local authority housing at more or less subsidised rents, of a free or poll-tax contributory health service, of extended facilities for public education, has revitalised the awareness of "need" as distinct from, and often as opposed to, "demand". The Seebohm Report in Britain, for instance, gave semi-official status to the idea that "the personal social services are large-scale experiments in ways of helping those in need".

Yet what is need? In the argument of the current poverty lobby in Britain, and above all of the writers associated with the Child Poverty Action Group, there has been a consistent tendency to stress individual need as something that the individual learns, and to worry away not only at Marshall's distinction between necessities of different kinds, but also at the distinction between necessities and what other conventional economists call "comforts" or even "luxuries". Undoubtedly the material basis for such a sustained intellectual offensive has been the non-market area of publicly provided social security.

A French study has made an effort to quantify the growth of this public sector need-provision. The Centre for Research and Documentation on Consumer Affairs (CREDOC) has identified three kinds of need: *elementary needs*, such as food, clothing, toiletries, etc.; *environmental needs*, such as housing, leisure, transport; and *"needs related to the person"*, such as education, sports, health, cultural provision. They then attempted to aggregate the expenditures in each category which were made in the open market, the cost of freely provided public services, and those other costs which were refunded by social security services. Their findings offer an interesting perspective:

	1959		1970	
	Collective Share	*Private Share*	*Collective Share*	*Private Share*
		(percentages)		
Elementary	0	100	0	100
Environmental	10	90	12.5	87.5
Person	54	46	68	32
All services	12	88	19	81

Of course, many questions remain to be asked within this framework. We cannot assume that these expenditures are uniform for all social groups, and the variations between one group and another can tell us extremely significant things about the social structure concerned.

What remains very clear is that public provision, taken at its own valuation, has different motors from market orientated production. Commonly the social services "create" or "discover" needs which hitherto had never been imagined by the governors of society, and possibly not even by some of the beneficiaries of the process. In the field of adult education, poor as it is in endowments, this is a truism. But it can also be held relevant in many other areas. In the newly formed British National Health Service, the original heavy demand for false teeth and spectacles triggered off a celebrated public controversy, once these items became

14

freely available. It was argued at the time that this rush for aid reflected the privation previously imposed by the system of market provision on those too poor (or too mean) to exercise "effective demand". But in a similar way the elaboration of medical technology constantly creates new and newer needs, some of them involving far more investment than teeth and glasses. No one could "need" a kidney machine until there was one.

Another interesting example is speech therapy. Roughly half a million people in Britain stammer (0.8% of the population). It has been calculated that perhaps four hundred thousand of these people are seriously afflicted. There are nine hundred full-time and five-hundred part-time speech therapists. A recent enquiry, published in the *Guardian*, asked thirty local education authorities how many adult classes they held for adult stammerers. It turned out that there were three adult evening classes in the whole country. As the author of this study points out:

> "This educational development is, therefore, in the hands of local stammerers and potential tutors, who must come out of their individual nonentity and organise themselves into a recognisable body."

"Need", that is to say, is not merely learned by imitation and diffused by social osmosis: awareness of it can be consciously communicated, the more so when remedies are on hand, but also to some extent when they are technically possible even if not actually available.

The emergence of "needs", and the means of meeting them in such a way, stands in sharp contrast to market demand stimulated by advertisements and accorded priority by the individual's purse. Inevitably, public provision raises problems about the allocation of scarce resources that call for new criteria and methods of settlement. In Britain, the Nottinghamshire County Council recently attracted serious adverse criticism when it appointed a "pocket-money advisor" to organise consumer advice for children in schools. The appointment was, of course, open to debate: although some at least of the consumer groups would have welcomed it. The question is, by what criteria should such decisions be made? How does one hitherto unrecognised "need" secure priority over another? Who decides, subject to what community controls?

Gunnar Myrdal, in his interesting study *Beyond the Welfare State*, points out that the institutions of welfare in the West have grown up in a democratic environment, in distinction from the mechanisms of planning in the USSR and other communist countries, which came into existence in the context of an authoritarian political framework. Unfortunately, however, the soil in which welfare has grown does not mean that it necessarily retains democratic properties itself. We have certainly not succeeded in rendering the public social services democratic in themselves, either in the sense of asserting direct popular participation in and control of them; or in the more fundamental and indispensable sense of subjecting them to effective and satisfying detailed public accountability. Indeed, there are many examples of the avowed purposes of social welfare institutions being stultified by centralisation and hierarchical organisation, and by the use of administrative criteria borrowed from enterprises whose objective is profitability in the market. Part of the problem can be seen in one of the most interesting studies of the taxonomy of need, published in *New Society* by Jonathan Bradshaw. Bradshaw is rightly concerned about the amorphousness of the concepts of need, and in an effort towards clarity separates four distinct definitions.

First, he identifies the idea of *normative* need, which may be summarised as the bureaucratic determination, by an administration or social scientists, of minimum levels of adequacy. These norms may be matched by remedial provision, or they may not. Examples he offers include the British Medical Association's nutritional standard, or Peter Townsend's "Incapacity Scale". Much progress has been made in defining such norms in the fields of housing and education during recent years.

Secondly, he recognises *felt* need, as the stated wants of those for whom services are offered.

Thirdly, he lists *expressed* need, or demand (not in the economic sense) in which the lack of something will provoke action, demanding a service. Examples he offers include hospital waiting lists or, possibly, housing waiting lists.

Finally, he accepts the idea of *comparative* need, in which either persons or areas are compared with others and found to lack amenities which are generally accepted as necessary elsewhere.

16

Bradshaw then goes on to offer a model connecting these different concepts: the model interrelates those more or less precise measures of need which may be elaborated on the basis of each one taken individually. The important thing about this whole valuable exercise is that it is directed exclusively at planners and policy makers, to enable them to refine and evaluate their judgements. And it is exactly this "need" of the planners which demonstrates how far our services are from being able to live up to Gunnar Myrdal's expectations about their "democratic" content, since effective participation and consultation would by themselves produce notable refinements in most public plans, as well as allowing planners to educate themselves in the process.

The relevance of this problem to the wider ecological issues, demanding as they do significant extensions of planning, in order to eke out scarce materials, to research and develop substitutes, and to clear up and prevent mess, should be evident. Democratic forms of society will be increasingly difficult to maintain unless we can effectively extend the principles of social accountability and direct popular participation in decision-making to what are, at present, either authoritarian or technocratic preserves. Naturally, this is not to argue against development of technique, which is no more urgent than ever, but to argue for its application to what people themselves regard as the most important issues, in response to democratic initiative under genuinely democratic control.

At this point, one must obviously consider the tools which are available for such controls. The growth of governmental and local administrative organs, voluntary organisations, trade unions, and pressure groups certainly provides us with a confusion of institutions. What is required is not simply a refinement of organisational forms, and still less a proliferation of offices in the hierarchy of bureaucratic institutions. It would be more fruitful to seek solutions in an enrichment of the simple traditional constitutional doctrine of the separation of powers, such as might prove possible once we began to take the notion of accountability seriously. Any genuine separation of powers exists to prevent the concentration of authority in a manner harmful to civil liberties. Bitter experience, in a succession of countries, reveals the peril of minimising the importance of the continuous extension of checks and controls to cope with the enormous growth of bureaucratic administrative forms. The fact that public provision for welfare needs, outside the "effective demand" of the market, could only be initiated through bureaucratic forms of administration in no way removes the necessity now to move towards democratic forms with all possible speed. Not to do so will result in waste of resources and the discrediting of welfare as a more advanced social objective than market efficiency.

In its pure form, this problem poses itself most clearly in the socialist societies, where planning is unimpeded by the institutions of private property, but where democratic initiatives are as yet markedly limited and, indeed, restricted. This has been perceptively understood by Mihailo Markovic, the Yugoslav scholar dismissed with his colleagues in the Belgrade School of Philosophy after an unprecedented governmental campaign culminating in an arbitrary decision by state authorities of Serbia to overrule the university statutes. At the beginning of 1975, against the will of their colleagues, the Belgrade Philosophers were suspended from teaching duties.

Markovic argues that the doctrine of separation of powers needs now to be consciously applied to information and communication services, so that not only raw data, but also access to competent and, if necessary, adverse technical advice, should become available to groups of citizens as of right, for whatever social purposes might be revelant to them.

In capitalist economies, the resistance to such doctrines has a dual root, in contrast to the single, bureaucratic-political source of limitations on the information flows which control the communist states. Capitalist societies encourage a certain dissociative pluralism in the communications media, and in the fields of intellectual organisation (although they have given rise to a bureaucracy in both local and national government and their out-stations, which is not without its East European parallel). But the major obstacle to freedom of information is still, in such societies, undoubtedly located in the institutions of private property, which require not only material producer goods but certain kinds of knowledge to be restricted to more or less exclusive proprietorship. Moreover, the outlook of private property and market needs dominates research and training in institutions of learning. To establish truly universal access to knowledge would be to negate the domination of resources by particular interests: and it is this salient fact which in the capitalist countries has encouraged the industrial demand for accountability, often pursued under the slogan "open the books".

Needless to say, this is not to argue that universal access to knowledge *can* be achieved without other prior material changes: George Orwell pinpointed this question with characteristic clarity when he wrote of the "proles": "Until they become conscious they will never rebel, and until after they have rebelled they cannot become conscious." While the problem is confined solely to human consciousness, it is insoluble.

So everything comes back to a deeper understanding of human needs in relation to social structures, to the theory to which Agnes Heller's work makes a basic contribution. The difficulty is to escape from the much repeated preconception that economics is coterminous with money and markets. This is the pen in which Professor Pigou, the author of the famous *The Economics of Welfare*, locked himself and three generations of academic economists concerned with "welfare". "Economic welfare", he wrote, ". . . is the subject matter of economic science". This, indeed, is what we all wish it to be. But it is rendered impossible immediately, by the terms of reference that he and the other economists impose upon themselves: "The range of our enquiry becomes restricted to that part of social welfare that can be brought directly or indirectly into relation with the measuring-rod of money." Socialists, including marxist socialists, have all eagerly tended to confine their vision with the same blinkers. They seem to have missed entirely the *critical motivation* that launched Marx on the study of the political economy of commodity production. *Capital* was "a critical analysis" of a structure of economic relationships doomed (whatever its temporary achievements as a springboard for future social development) to fail as a stable structure capable of meeting the human needs of human beings.

Ken Coates and Stephen Bodington

"Laugh if you wish at the dreamer
Who saw flowers bloom in midwinter."
(Franz Schubert and Wilhelm Müller: "Frühlingstraum", from
Die Winterreise)

NOTE ON THE METHOD OF PRESENTATION

In the following work, Marx's theory of need is analysed on the basis of his main writings, not of the contents of all his writings. The well-versed reader will be able to find observations in Marx's titanic life's work that contradict some of my own statements or inferences. This is quite inevitable, since even in his main works (as we shall see later) Marx does not use a wholly precise terminology, and he sometimes offers several interpretations or jots down ideas which are only momentary. I am quite sure that there is no such thing as an interpretation of Marx which is proof against being "contradicted" by means of quotations. But I have put the word "contradicted" in quotation marks quite intentionally. What interests me is the main tendency (or tendencies) of his thought, and I have tried to examine these in relation to the given problem.

I

Preliminary Observations on Marx's Concept of Need

When Marx summarised what was original in his economic discoveries by comparison with classical political economy, he listed the following theoretical points:

1) The theory that the worker sells to the capitalist not his labour but his labour power.

2) An elaboration of the general category of surplus value, and the demonstration that profit, interest and ground rent are merely phenomenal forms of surplus value.

3) The discovery of the significance of use value. (Marx points out that the categories value and exchange value are not new but are taken over from classical political economy.)

An analysis of these three discoveries which Marx attributes to himself will show that in some way they are built upon the concept of need.

First, let us examine use value. Marx defines the commodity as use value in the following way: "A commodity is . . . a thing that by its properties satisfies human needs of some sort or another."[1] In this context it is irrelevant whether the needs are in the stomach or in the imagination. Satisfaction of a need is the *sine qua non* of any commodity. There is no value (exchange value) without use value (satisfaction of needs), but use values (goods) may well exist without value (exchange value), as long as they satisfy needs (which is precisely the definition of use values). It needs to be made clear from the outset that Marx uses the concept of need in order to make definitions, but that he never actually defines the concept of need itself. On no occasion does he describe what is to be understood by the term "need".

Use value, then, is defined directly in terms of needs. This is also true (indirectly, perhaps, but in just as many parts of his work) of the idea that the worker sells his labour power to the capitalist: he gives use value and, in return, receives exchange

23

value. What is it that determines the value which he receives, i.e. the value of labour power? We know the answer: the value of the means of subsistence necessary for the reproduction of labour power. The quantity of value which corresponds to a given level of productivity is in turn fixed by the needs of the worker. The totality of his needs for mere survival (including the maintenance of children) represents the lowest limit. However, on more than one occasion Marx speaks of the historicity of these needs, their dependence on tradition, the cultural level etc. (we shall come back to this point).

The worker, then, sells his labour power, i.e. a use value, to the capitalist. As we have seen, use value by definition satisfies needs: the need for the production of surplus value and for the valorisation [*Bewertung*] of capital. (If labour power did not produce surplus value and the capitalist did not buy labour power, the capitalist relation would cease to operate.) "The law of capitalistic accumulation, metamorphosed by economists into a pretended law of Nature, in reality merely states that the very nature of accumulation excludes every diminution in the degree of exploitation of labour and every rise in the price of labour, which could seriously imperil the continual reproduction, on an ever enlarging scale, of the capitalistic relation. It cannot be otherwise in a mode of production in which the labourer exists to satisfy *the needs of self-expansion of existing values** instead of, on the contrary, material wealth existing to satisfy the *needs of development* on the part of the labourer."[2]

For the present, let us simply bear in mind that the statement that material wealth ought to serve the worker's needs of development is based squarely on *a non-economic choice of values*. But let us turn back now to the category of surplus value. We have seen that the production of surplus value satisfies a need (the "need" to valorise capital). But Marx also defines the *possibility* of producing surplus value in terms of needs. Throughout Marx's writing there runs the idea that the possibility of producing surplus value comes about when a given society is capable of producing more than enough to satisfy its own "vital needs". To be sure, Marx does not say that produc-

---

* Here and throughout the book, the italics in the passages quoted from Marx are Agnes Heller's.

tion of surplus value comes about in every such situation, but
only that it is not possible without this surplus. The question of
when the production of surplus value takes place and when it
does not is a specific problem, a function of the interaction of
innumerable factors.

From the standpoint of its historical origins, the production of
surplus value establishes and reproduces private property and
the division of labour (which, at least in its origins, is the same
thing). The development of the division of labour and thus of
productivity creates not only material wealth but a wealth and
diversity of needs. It is because of the division of labour that
needs too are "divided": the position of need within the division
of labour determines the structure of need, or at least its limits.
This contradiction reaches its peak in capitalism and becomes,
as we shall see, the greatest antinomy in the antinomy-system of
this society.

We can see, then, that in the new economic discoveries which
Marx regarded as his own, the concept of need plays one of the
main roles, if not actually *the* main role. One only has to look
at the categories which he consciously passed over to realise that
need plays no part in them. Classical political economy did not
attribute any importance to use value, which therefore presented
it with no problems: the worker sells his labour to the capitalist,
but both the aspects of this act that relate to needs are missing.
And when profit, interest and ground rent enter the discussion,
no reference to needs appears here either.

Of course, this does not mean that the concept of "need"
played no part in classical political economy: on the contrary,
it could even be said to have been a decisive concept. But the
perspective and the context are entirely different from Marx's.
The analysis and assessment of need are developed from the
point of view of capitalism, and they are therefore purely
economic: economic value is the only value, the highest of all
values, and cannot be transcended from any other point of view.
The needs of the worker appear as *limits* of wealth and are
analysed as such. At the same time, however, the need that
appears in the form of effective demand is a motive force and a
means of economic development. In the *Economic and Philosophic Manuscripts of 1844*, Marx is already passionately reject-

Redefinition g Treatment
Redefinition g Practice

ing the purely economic concept of need as resulting from the standpoint of capitalism. With regard to political economy, he writes: "Everything that goes beyond the most abstract need — be it in the realm of passive enjoyment or a manifestation of activity — seems to him [the economist] a luxury."[3] And further on: "Society, as it appears to the political economist, is civil society, in which every individual is a totality of needs and only exists for the other person, as the other exists for him, in so far as each becomes a means for the other."[4] (The negative tone is quite unequivocal: it is based on the kantian imperative, by which man should not be a mere means for other men.) According to Marx, the reduction of the concept of need to economic need is an expression of the (capitalist) alienation of needs, in a society in which the goal of production is not the satisfaction of needs but the valorisation of capital, in which the system of needs is constituted from the division of labour and need appears only on the market, in the form of effective demand.

Later, we shall examine the structure of need in the society of "associated producers" which Marx presents to us. Here we want to draw attention only to one aspect of it: the society of "associated producers" cannot be distinguished from capitalism by a constant increase in productivity. In such a society, the increase in production is correlated with the quantity (and quality) of the use value: the "material wealth" of society advances, it satisfies and at the same time produces needs. It bears no direct relationship to the production of value (exchange value), because this relates to the necessary labour time (see Marx, *Capital*, Vol. 1, page 45). Through the mediation of the law of value, however, the increase in productivity *can* also be related to needs; by this law, the socially necessary labour time is diminished, with the consequent possibiilty for the worker of satisfying a "higher level" of needs. But according to Marx, this can never come about in capitalism, partly because the valorisation of capital sets a limit to the reduction of labour time, and partly because (and we shall see that this is the decisive factor) no structure of need can be built *ab ovo* that will enable ordinary people to use their free time to satisfy "higher needs". This possibility can be realised only in the society of "associated producers". That is, a society where needs do not appear on the market, where the primary emphasis goes on the evaluation of needs and of the corresponding allocation

26

of labour power and labour time; a society where the whole structure of need changes (with labour itself becoming a vital need), where people share goods according to their needs, and where the primary needs are not those relating to material goods but those directed towards "higher activities", and above all those directed towards other people, who are seen not as means but as ends.

Now it should no longer appear to be an accident that the concept of need plays the hidden but principal role in Marx's economic categories, just as it is no accident that the concept of need is not defined in his critiques of political economy and capitalism. Marx's categories of need (we shall see that he gives several interpretations of it) are *not* as a whole economic categories. He tends to treat concepts of need as non-economic categories, as historical-philosophical, that is as anthropological value categories, and therefore as not subject to definition within the economic system. In order to be able to analyse the economic categories of capitalism as categories of alienated needs (e.g. the need to valorise capital, the system of need imposed by the division of labour, the continuous appearance of needs on the market, the limitation of the workers' needs to "the necessary means of existence", the manipulation of needs), it is necessary to create the positive category of a "system of non-alienated needs", the full evolution and realisation of which we place at a future point when the economy itself will also be subordinated to this "human" system of needs.

Before making a clear examination of Marx's whole philosophical conception of need, let us briefly see what various interpretations he applies to this concept. There is no philosophical or economic work of importance by Marx in which he does not repeatedly try, often in several different passages, to classify types of need. The classification is made sometimes from a historical-philosophical or anthropological point of view, sometimes on the basis of ways in which needs are objectified, sometimes from the economic standpoint (particularly in the analysis of supply and demand), and sometimes by the consciously valorising application of the value category "human wealth". We should add that almost all these classifications contain the aspect of value judgement, even

27

when a value category is not directly used as a basis for classification.

The very classification of these various points of view indicates a certain heterogeneity. There would be no inherent difficulty in describing Marx's position if the different standpoints were always made explicitly distinct. However, the "points of view" themselves are often ambiguous and unclear. This is particularly so because quite often the valorising attitude is not conscious. Moreover, in his classification of economic needs, philosophical concepts often prevail and, last but not least, the *status quo* of capitalist society often influences the historical-philosophical-anthropological classification. This, and not any lingering feuerbachism, is the reason why Marx does not go beyond the naturalistic concept of need, though he often tries to do so.

The most problematical point is the classification of needs on the basis of their objectifications, that is to say, on the basis of their objects in general, and of their respective activities, feelings and passions. (We shall see, in the course of analysing the philosophical concept of need, that Marx considered the object of need and the need itself to be always interrelated.) Types of need are formed in accordance with the objects towards which they are directed and the activities involving those objects. Marx's most general classification in this sense is between "material" and "spiritual" goods, although he also mentions political needs, the needs of social life and the needs of labour (activity). In this classification, the value judgement is not a general, sustained standpoint. The satisfaction of material needs is not only the basic condition of human existence, the expansion of material needs is at the same time a sign of the "enrichment" of man; however, there is still a certain "spiritual need" which can be alienated. The value judgement affects the totality of the structure of need: we shall return to this point later. Of course there are individual passages from Marx where a different emphasis in one or another direction can be found, but this is always only functional to the examination of the *problem*, and one cannot draw conclusions from such passages relating to the totality of his conception.

The historical-philosophical-anthropological classification is based on two categories, that of "natural" needs and that of "socially produced" needs (the first are synonymous with "physical" or "necessary" needs; the second correspond to

28

"social" needs, at least in the applied sense of the word). How does Marx interpret these needs?

In the *Economic and Philosophic Manuscripts of 1844*, he writes: "Man produces even when he is free from physical need and only truly produces in freedom therefrom."[5] Physical needs correspond here to biological needs, which are directed towards maintenance of the mere conditions of life. Marx (despite the appearance of the terminology) separates himself here from the naturalistic interpretation, as he does in many of his mature writings. This is not only the case when he is speaking about a radically new human-social content in animal-biological needs (a content which, apart from one or two formulations, is quite clear in Marx later on). It is also the case when he is considering the *reduction of "human" needs to needs which, though they have a social content, are of a* bio-psychological "nature", a product of capitalist society. It is bourgeois society that subordinates the human senses to "crude, practical needs" and makes them "abstract" by reducing them to mere needs of survival. For this reason, needs aimed merely at survival cannot form a general, historical-philosphical group of needs which is independent.

Later, as a consequence of the economic point of view, a classification becomes necessary which, more or less modified (that is, with a different interpretation), appears in the writings of his maturity: the distinction between "natural" and "socially produced" needs. As I have already said, the economic point of view is an explanation of the origin of surplus labour and surplus value and of the possibility of their existence. But it is also motivated by the *status quo* in capitalist society as the point of departure for marxist analysis, and by the discovery of exploitation as the leading motive in the critique of capitalism.

We ought now to concern ourselves with the contexts in which these categories appear (we shall underline the most important aspects). In the *Grundrisse* Marx speaks of "the capacity to consume" as the creator of needs in capitalist society, and distinguishes the needs "created by society" from "natural" needs.[6] In the same work, regarding capitalism, he says:

"Capital's ceaseless striving towards the general form of wealth drives labour beyond the limits of its natural paltryness, and thus creates the material elements for the development of

29

the rich individuality which is as all-sided in its production as in its consumption and whose labour also therefore appears no longer as labour but as the full development of activity itself in which natural necessity in its direct form has disappeared; because a historically created need has taken the place of the natural one."[7]

And further on:

"Luxury is the opposite of the naturally necessary. Necessary needs are those of the individual himself reduced to a natural subject. The development of industry suspends this natural necessity as well as this former luxury — in bourgeois society, it is true, it does so only in antithetical form, in that it itself only posits another specific social standard as necessary, opposite luxury."[8]

In *Capital*, the category ("natural needs") appears in relation to the determination of the value of labour power:

"His natural needs, such as food, clothing, fuel, and housing, vary according to the climatic and other physical conditions of his country. On the other hand, the number and extent of his so-called necessary needs, as also the modes of satisfying them, are themselves the product of historical development, and depend therefore to a great extent on the degree of civilisation of a country, more particularly on the conditions under which, and consequently on the habits and degree of comfort in which, the class of free labourers has been formed. In contradistinction therefore to the case of other commodities, there enters into the determination of the value of labour power a historical and moral element."[9]

Finally, the value of labour power is defined as follows:

"The value of labour power is determined by the value of the necessaries of life habitually required by the average labourer."[10]

The classification given appears here for the first time. On the difference between the value of labour power in different countries, Marx also writes:

"In the comparison of the wages in different nations, we must therefore take into account all the factors that determine changes in the amount of the value of labour power; the price and the extent of the prime necessaries of life as naturally and historically developed."[11]

For the analysis of this question I would refer again to Marx's

30

statement that material production has always been the realm of necessity and will remain so even in the society of "associated producers".[12] With the development of the productive forces, "This realm of physical necessity expands as a result of his needs."[13]

From all these quotations, it would appear that the category of "natural needs" — at least from the *Grundrisse* through to the third volume of *Capital* — has not changed its meaning, but that there has been a change in the concept of "necessary needs".

Let us first analyse the group of "natural needs". "Natural needs" refer to the simple maintenance of human life (self-preservation), and are "naturally necessary" simply because, without satisfying them, man is not able to preserve himself as a mere natural being. These needs are not identical with those of animals, because for his own self-preservation man must also have certain conditions (warmth, clothing) for which the animal has no "need". The necessary needs for sustaining man as a natural being are therefore also social (there is a well-known passage in the *Grundrisse* according to which the hunger that is satisfied with knife and fork is different from the hunger which is satisfied by raw meat): the mode of satisfaction makes the need itself social. Nevertheless, there is a contradiction between the concept of "natural needs" (as an independent "group of needs", and the concept of "social" or "socially produced" needs; or at the very least, there is something which cannot be coherently integrated into Marx's philosophical theory of need. Let us now examine needs as *structure of need* (later on we shall see that Marx himself does this). If we state that the structure of need as a whole can only be interpreted in its correlation with the totality of social relations (and a quotation from Marx's *The Poverty of Philosophy* will prove this point), then it follows that only socially produced needs exist, and "natural needs" (whose mode of satisfaction changes the need itself) also have this "socially produced" character.

According to Marx, as we have seen, industrial production makes it possible to resolve the opposition between "natural" needs and "socially produced" needs, even if in capitalist society this takes place in a contradictory way, and even if this society — temporarily — reproduces the contradiction. The overcoming

31

of the contradiction between "natural" and "socially produced" needs is thus a result of the pushing back of the natural limits. The pushing back of the objective and subjective natural limits is interrelated: Marx does not distinguish between internal and external nature. If, however, on the basis of this perceptive thought, it is unnecessary to establish an independent group of "natural needs", then it is also true that external nature exists for man only in reciprocal interaction with society, in the process of socialisation, in the organic exchange between man and nature.

While the group of "natural needs" is not open to interpretation within the philosophy of Marx as a whole, the idea that Marx wished to express with the creation of this group is however plausible and simple. It is only industrial production and the capitalist development of productivity that definitively (in Marx's terms: irrevocably) cause the maintenance of sheer physical existence to cease to be a special problem and goal, shaping the practice of man's daily life; people no longer work solely to fill their own stomachs and those of their children, and to protect themselves and their families from death by exposure.

The development of industrial production not only provides an opportunity to satisfy "natural needs" fully but, where possible, does away with the problem (the contradiction) once and for all. The *Economic and Philosophic Manuscripts of 1844* contain the profound insight that strictly speaking it is capitalist society which executes the reduction to "physical needs", which in other words constitutes the independent group of "natural needs". In the later works, this appears as the capitalist reproduction of the contradiction. There can be no doubt that this shift of emphasis gives expression to a more positive value relation (value judgement) to the capitalist mode of production.

Of course, the tabulation of this separate group of "natural needs" does not mean, in our view, that this concept is organically rooted in Marx's general philosophical theory of need, nor that we would maintain such a "grouping" in a marxist theory of need today. In our view the "natural needs" are not a group of needs but a limit concept: a limit (different for different societies) beyond which human life is no longer reproducible as such, beyond which the limit of bare existence is passed (mass deaths from famine in India and Pakistan show exactly this). It would be sheer élitism, at least in our world, to eliminate this limit concept from the discussion of man's needs. Therefore I shall speak not of "natural needs" but of the "existential limit to the satisfaction of needs".

We noted that the meaning of "necessary needs" undergoes a change between the *Grundrisse* and *Capital*. In the *Grundrisse* they correspond fully to natural needs, but in *Capital* the difference is stressed. "Necessary" needs *develop*, historically, they are not dictated by mere survival; the cultural element in such needs, the moral element and custom, are decisive, and their satisfaction is an organic part of the "normal" life of people belonging to a particular class in a given society. The quantum which we refer to as the "necessary articles or means for survival" at a given time or for a given class serves to satisfy vital needs and "necessary needs".

In this interpretation the concept of "necessary needs" is especially important, even though it is simply a descriptive concept. If we investigate empirically what needs ought to be satisfied so that the members of a given society or class should have the feeling and the conviction that their life — at a given level of the division of labour — is "normal", then we arrive at the concept of "necessary needs". The extent and the content of necessary needs can therefore be different in different periods and for different classes. For a worker in the United States today, "necessary needs" mean something different from the needs of an English worker in the time of Marx or those of an Indian worker today. Marx also has something to say about needs in this sense in *The Poverty of Philosophy*, when he points to a contradiction between a worker's needs and his possibilities. This means that the necessary needs of the worker cannot be satisfied because they are not covered by effective demand.

We have already said that we consider the category of "necessary needs" as a descriptive concept of exceptional importance which is relevant sociologically, so to speak. However, its philosophical content evaporates precisely because of the descriptive character of the concept. When Marx speaks of the "necessary needs" of English workers in his day, he means by this not only material needs, but also those of a non-material kind that may be explained in the concept of "the average". Education also appears amongst these categories, as well as books and membership of a trade union. But since the satisfaction of these needs (at a given time and under given circumstances) depends upon material means and is "purchasable" with money (in the case of membership of a trade union, Marx is referring to the trade union subscription), they must be considered as "necessary", and the amount of value spent in satisfying them includes the value of the labour power. However, *individual* needs do not belong to this category; such needs cannot be "average" and in particular their satisfaction is not "purchasable". So some needs which are alike fall into different categories (meat comes into the category of necessary needs, artichokes into that of luxury needs); on the other hand, some needs that are different in kind fall into the same category (whisky and trade union subscriptions are necessary needs).

When, however, Marx defines the characteristics of "necessary needs" not empirically but philosophically from the standpoint of *content* he reaches quite different results. The realm of material production is — and remains so in the society of "associated producers" — the realm of necessity. In this sense "necessary needs" are the needs that are constantly growing out of material production. In the society of "associated producers", *material needs* (in consumption and production) have to be measured, and the labour power as well as the labour time which corresponds to it have to be distributed. In this context and on the basis of this interpretation, spiritual and moral needs, those that relate to the collectivity, are the opposite of necessary needs. Such needs will not be fixed — at least in the future — by their position in the division of labour, because they are *individual* needs (they cannot be expressed by any average), and because their satisfaction is not purchasable (all the more so, since there will be no money).

These would thus be the so-called "free" needs, a characteristic peculiar to the "realm of freedom".

Let us turn briefly again to the problem of the naturalistic determination of "natural needs". Since need for Marx, as we have already seen, is a kind of subject-object correlation, it is obvious that the problem also occurs from the point of view of the *object* (the object of the need) — that is, from the point of view of use value. The naturalistic interpretation of needs presupposes a naturalistic interpretation of use value, just as the

34

superseding of the former presupposes the superseding of the latter.

With regard to this problem, all we can do is to indicate a tendency; it so happens that Marx gives different interpretations in one and the same work. In *Capital*, use value is defined as the "natural form" of the commodity, which expresses the relation between the individual and nature. (This same definition is to be found in the economic manuscripts of 1857/58.) In *Theories of Surplus Value* a similar naturalistic conception is to be found, indeed it goes further: "Use value expresses the natural relation between things and men, the existence of things for men. Exchange value is . . . the social existence of the thing." However, in the same volume there is the following statement: "The autonomous material form of wealth disappears and does not appear again except as a manifestation of man. Everything that is not the result of a human activity, of labour, is nature and as such is not social wealth. The phantom of the world of commodities disappears and does not reappear except as a constantly disappearing and constantly regenerated objectification of human labour."

If we now investigate the manner in which Marx grouped needs together from the economic point of view (according to supply and demand) we shall, albeit not definitively, move away from the conceptions discussed above. In Marx the groups of needs which are respectively "necessary" and "luxury" needs, or "true" and "luxury" needs, or "true" and "imaginary" needs, do not always and unconditionally have an economic meaning. (The coupled phrase "natural needs — luxury needs" appears only in the *Grundrisse*, where Marx, as we have seen, does not yet distinguish the former from "necessary needs"). The division which can be interpreted unambiguously only by means of the economic categories also contains, generally speaking, historical-philosophical elements and very often carries a valorising emphasis. The question is, whether it is possible to categorise needs (or the objects towards which they are directed) on the basis of their content and their quality, along with the categories of necessity and luxury, or whether it is solely and primarily effective demand that decides whether a need and the object related to it are a "luxury".

In *The Poverty of Philosophy* the two solutions are not sufficiently distinguished. It must be admitted that Marx inclines towards the purely economic interpretation. In his polemic with Proudhon's conception that the most used objects are at the same time the most useful (and according to which spirits ought for example to be classed as one of the most useful consumer goods!), Marx makes the point that production decides on the concrete content of necessary needs: the more labour power is employed in the manufacture of an article the more it approximates to the group of luxury products. In the same work there also appears a non-economic definition that contradicts this interpretation. Marx writes as follows: "The most indispensable objects, like corn, meat, etc., rise in price, while cotton, sugar, coffee, etc., fall to a surprising degree. And even among comestibles proper, the luxury articles, like artichokes, asparagus, etc., are today relatively cheaper than foodstuffs of prime necessity. In our age, the superfluous is easier to produce than the necessary."[14] However, in this interpretation "luxury products" or "luxury needs" are no longer an economic category; they appear instead as the counterpart of the descriptive sociological concept of "necessary needs", and "moral" elements and "historical" elements, custom etc. play an incisive role. In this case, luxury needs are all those things that by custom do not belong to the system of need of the labour force. The economic interpretation, by contrast, considers something a luxury article if its object (possession, consumption of the object) lies beyond the power of acquisition of the working class. In this latter sense it cannot be said that luxury products become cheap, but only that the product which becomes cheaper than others used for similar purposes is no longer a luxury product. (It can be shown with examples that this has come about in a *de facto* way: today sugar and artichokes are certainly not luxury goods.)

Similar problems are posed in relation to this same classification in the second volume of *Capital*, where consumer goods are subdivided in the following way:

(1) "Consumer necessities, regardless of whether such a product as tobacco is really a consumer necessity from the physiological point of view. It suffices that it is habitually such"; and,

(2) "Articles of luxury, which enter into the consumption of

only the capitalist class and can therefore be exchanged only for spent surplus value, which never falls to the share of the labourer."[15]

I believe that this is the only relevant interpretation for determining what are luxury products and luxury needs; it is concretely applied in concrete situations.

No specific product or need *possesses* the quality of being a luxury product or a luxury need. That is determined solely by the question of whether the object is possessed and used (and therefore the corresponding need is satisfied) by the majority of the population or only by that minority which represents a significantly higher level of purchasing power as a result of the social division of labour. As a consequence of increasing productivity, and as a consequence of changes in the social structure, needs that originally were luxury needs become necessary needs, without their undergoing the slightest qualitative modification. (The opposite may also happen. Marx had already drawn attention to the fact that at the beginning of the process of capitalist reproduction in England a part of what had earlier been necessary needs became luxury needs.) So this is the marxist concept that I accept, and I think the category of "luxury needs" can only be interpreted in an economic sense.

We shall refer to this problem later on. On the phase of prosperity in capitalism, Marx writes as follows: "The working class . . . also enjoys momentarily articles of luxury ordinarily beyond its reach."[16] But the moment there is effective demand from the working class, this demand does not satisfy "luxury needs": in accordance with what has been said above, such needs cease to be luxury needs. This ambiguity in the concepts of "luxury products" and "luxury needs" is not at variance with Marx's general conception, by which the whole population can enjoy such "luxury needs" only in exceptional and brief periods. Prosperity is followed by crisis: the same articles (and satisfaction of the needs related to them) are once more unattainable. With the hindsight of experience of capitalist development, it might rather be said (as Marx in any case always maintained) that every society founded upon the division of labour reproduces these economically separate groups of needs (necessary needs and luxury needs). Only the society of associated producers can overcome this opposition, not only because the so-called "luxury needs" cease to exist, but also because the system of "necessary needs" itself changes, opening the way for the development of individual "free needs". What we are arguing against is simply the idea that "luxury needs" are definable in terms of their content and their quality, and that needs in general can be subdivided into "necessary needs" and "luxury needs" on the basis of their concrete quality or quantity.

Fixed, concrete valorising categories appear also in the above-mentioned groups. Marx may have referred just once to "real" and "imaginary" use values, but the main tendency is to eliminate valorising categories.

Nevertheless, the basis and yardstick of any regrouping or classification is *need as a category of value.*

For Marx here, as on other occasions, the most important category of value is that of wealth; at the same time, this constitutes a critique of the use that classical political economy made of the category "wealth", in identifying it with material wealth. For Marx, the precondition of "human" wealth is only the basis for the free development of all the capacities and senses of the human being, the free and many-sided activity of every individual. Need as a category of value is none other than the need for this kind of wealth. In the *Economic and Philosophic Manuscripts of 1844* Marx writes: "It will be seen how in place of the wealth and poverty of political economy comes the rich human being and the rich human need. The rich human being is simultaneously the human being in need *of a totality of human manifestations of life.*"[17] And later on: "Private property does not know how to change the crude need into human need."[18] Marx rejects the society of private and capitalist property, making his point of departure the value of "rich human need". Private property is incapable of transforming "crude needs" into "rich human needs", however great the material riches that it produces.

The elaboration of the category of value "need" is the work of the young Marx. In his maturity this category is already a given point of departure: he does not consider it necessary to analyse it anew. Nevertheless, it frequently appears later on, in a direct and open form. Let us recall the quotation in which Marx contrasts the need to valorise capital with the worker's "needs of development" or, at its most clearcut, the concept of "radical needs", which also functions as a category of value (we shall

38

deal later on with this concept and the key role which it plays in Marx's theory).

However, these "pure" concepts of value are often found not only as the basis but as the concluding point in the critique of capitalism. "There are not too many necessities of life produced, in proportion to the existing population. Quite the reverse. Too little is produced to *decently* and *humanely* satisfy the wants of the great mass."[19]

But one does not need to fall back on examples of pure categories of value in order to demonstrate that every judgement concerning needs is measured on the basis of the positive value of "rich human needs". What else could have served as Marx's basis for rejecting the bifurcation between luxury needs and "necessary" needs? How else could he have denounced a society which creates wealth on the one hand and poverty on the other? By what other criterion could an economic structure be condemned, if not because its dynamic is motivated by the need to valorise capital rather than by the worker's needs of development? On what other basis could Marx have opposed, to the realm of material production as the realm of necessity, another realm: that of free self-activity, of freedom? Why otherwise would he have had such a high regard, as a positive model of the future, for "free time devoted to many-sided activity" and for the raising of labour to meet the needs of life, always using leisure as the yardstick of the real wealth of society? How otherwise could he have asserted the positive character of the *individual property* that comes with the disappearance of private property and the distribution of goods according to *individual* needs? Bernstein's penetrating scrutiny discerned the "value judgement" in Marx's attitude and sought to remove it from the economic analysis of capitalist society — when in fact the two aspects are inseparable. Without premises of value Marx's work would be a merely implicit critique of capitalism, lacking an inherent investigation into the nature of capitalism: he would be an anti-capitalist romantic.

II

The General Philosophical Concept of Needs and the Alienation of Needs

Marx develops the general philosophical concept of need in the *Economic and Philosophic Manuscripts of 1844* and in *The German Ideology*. In the following exposition we shall therefore where possible refer to these works. Some of the problems are not taken up again in the later works, at least not in a systematic manner. Others are presented in his mature writings with various modified interpretations. Where there are sufficiently clear indications of changes in Marx's thought (which appear particularly in the *Grundrisse*), we shall contrast them with the ideas of the young Marx.

Man's need and the object of the need are correlated: the need is always related to some concrete object or to an objective activity. The objects "bring about" the needs, and the needs bring about the objects. The need and its object are "moments", "sides" of one and the same complex. But if we analyse not one static model but the dynamic of a "social body" (presupposing that this "social body" has a dynamic), then the moment of production occupies first place: it is production which creates new needs. Certainly, the production that creates new needs is also correlated with the needs that are already present: "the various shaping of material life is, of course, in every case dependent on the needs which are already developed, and the production, as well as the satisfaction, of these needs is a historical process."[20]

Naturally, the "object" of need is not restricted in its meaning the objectivity of material things. The world in its totality is an objective world; every social relation, every social product is the objectivation of man. (Later on, Marx makes a basic distinction between objectivation [*Objektivation*] and objectification [*Vergegenständlichung*]. However, this does not indicate any modification of the theory of need.) In the process of objectification of

40

man, the human senses come about; it is the already present objectified human condition that develops human senses and needs in every man, at least as far as possible: "Thus, the objectification of the human essence, *both in its theoretical and practical aspects,* is required to make a man's sense human, as well as to create the human sense corresponding to the entire wealth of human and natural substance."[21] The highest object of human need is the other person. In other words: the measure in which man has become the highest object of need for other men determines the level of humanisation of human needs.

Animal needs, too, are always directed towards objects. But animal needs and their objects are "given" by the biological constitution of the animal. They can indeed be developed, but only as regards their manner of satisfaction. As the natural limits recede, however, human needs are increasingly orientated towards objectification (in the sense of activity as well as in the sense of "objectivation"). Man creates the objects of his need and, at the same time, the means for satisfying it (these two can correspond with each other, but not unconditionally). The history of man's origins is, at root, the history of the origins of his needs.

This theory of "genesis" is to be found twice in Marx's work, in two neighbouring passages of *The German Ideology*: "the first historical act is thus the production of the means to satisfy these needs [i.e. animal needs]." And shortly afterwards: ". . . and this production of new needs is the first historical act."[22] Between them, these quotations express the same thought from two different points of view. In so far as we create tools to satisfy our needs, the need for tools is already a new need, different from animal need. The poetic expression "the first historical act" therefore describes the creation of new needs and qualities of need not given in man's biological constitution.

Human need therefore comes about in the process of objectification; the objects of need "guide" and "steer" man, who is born in human society, in the formation of his needs. The needs are, in a general sense, "abandoned" in the course of their objectivation and in the objectified world, and the objectifying activities bring about new needs. The orientation of needs towards objects also points to the *active* character of needs. Needs are simultaneously passions and capacities (the passion and capacity to appropriate the object) and thus *capacities are themselves*

41

needs. The capacity for objective activity is thus one of the greatest needs of man. (This philosophical conception is the very foundation, and subsequently the determining factor, in Marx's conception of the development of labour into a "vital need".)

In general, we can call "need" only that human need which is related to objectivation and guided by it. In the case of animals one speaks of necessity, instinct, "drive", etc. This is of course merely a question of definition; it is important for us only because of the decisive role it plays in the analysis of the socialised psyche (e.g. in the analysis of what, like needs, guides human instincts and "drives" as well as the desires, passions and longings which are orientated towards the individual objects of needs). In the animal it is not possible to draw this kind of distinction between "attitude towards the object" and the individual object of its "drive". Need as demand, "created" by the "objectifications" themselves and orientated towards qualitatively different classes of objects, and the individual desire (guided by these needs) for concrete specimens of such objects (the former can be seen as a value relationship, the latter cannot), are a complex phenomenon. In it, the specifically historical-anthropological application of the concept of need appears to be not very significant. This does not only apply to those needs or desires which are perfectly "free" from biological motives. The sexual need directed towards a mother has for many thousands of years stood in opposition to the social norms of sexual need (and to the value relation inherent in the need) — otherwise it would not have created a "complex" (in the psychological sense of the word). In this case, the objects of the need (and thus the needs themselves) are socially or, as a result of interiorisation, individually "abandoned" for the biological motive which functions in a *universal* way (e.g. drives such as sex or hunger). Do not think that we are digressing from the analysis of Marx's thought. In fact, Marx takes the trouble on several occasions to distinguish needs from the desires directed towards concrete "objects".

In his investigation of the psychological relation to needs (that is, the psychological aspect of need), Marx appears essentially as a "man of the Enlightenment", and his thinking is akin to Fourier's. In *The German Ideology*, during an attack on Stirner, he writes:

"Whether a desire becomes fixed or not . . . depends on

whether material circumstances . . . allow of this desire being satisfied *normally* and, on the other hand, of the development of a whole mass of desires. This latter depends, in turn, on whether we live in circumstances that allow all round activity and thereby the full development of all our potentialities."[23]

In a passage later crossed out in the manuscript of the same work, he examines this problem in depth. We think it right to refer to this quotation here, since Marx undoubtedly still held to the position that he expressed there. The line of argument corresponds in all essentials to what was adopted in the final drafting, and is expressed in the following terms:

"Communist organisation has a two-fold effect on the desires produced in the individual by present day conditions; some of these desires — namely those existing under all conditions, which only change their form and direction under different social conditions — are merely altered by the communist social system, for they are given the opportunity to develop *normally*; others however — namely those originating in a particular social system, . . . — are totally deprived of their conditions of existence."[24]

So Marx speaks of "desires" which are fixed and irremovable [*nicht aufhebbar*], those in fact which are based on biological motives, and he goes on to note that "communists only strive to achieve an organisation of production and intercourse which will make possible the normal satisfaction of all needs, i.e. a satisfaction which is limited only by the needs themselves."[25]

Let us note first that the expression "normal" plays a decisive role in all three quotations. ("Normality" often functions in Marx as a criterion of value; the *Introduction to a Critique of Political Economy* comes to mind, where Marx speaks of ancient Greece as the "normal" infancy of humanity.) If man is rich in needs, and if the satisfaction of his needs is limited only by other needs, then desires are channelled along a "normal" course; they are not fixed exclusively on a single object and thus can be satisfied "normally".

Marx does not return elsewhere to the psychological aspect of needs; but on this question he clearly never gave up his rationalist, "enlightenment" point of view. The point is not only that he assumes that in the society of associated producers the structure of the psyche and of consciousness will be profoundly *different* from that of the present, but also that he never questions this *possibility* or the process itself; nor does he raise the question of the tempo of this change in psyche. So long as men are changing society, they are also radically changing themselves; it is a "natural" (that is, "normal") process, whose outcome is never in doubt.

To prevent misunderstanding, I would like to make it clear that I do not wish to defend the notion of "eternal human nature". In communism there is already an affirmation of the possibility that the human psyche should change radically in the process of overcoming alienation. However, on the one hand this process is much longer and more complicated than Marx thought; and, on the other, I do not think that a society (and a human psyche) can exist in which a collision between desires and needs is impossible. The fact that only other needs place limits on the satisfaction of needs still does not assert anything about the relation between passions and needs. The prediction that only other needs will place limits on needs may be true of the reciprocal relationship between *satisfiable* needs (although in this case too there might be doubts about which needs limit which others); but this view may not be universally valid, because "material" needs are limited by production whilst other needs are limited by the most diverse and heterogeneous "objects".

The problem of the alienation of needs constitutes the centre of Marx's philosophical analysis of needs. Here too, as we have seen, the criterion of value is man "rich in needs". The alienation of needs is equivalent to alienation of this wealth.

"Man rich in needs" is thus a consciously philosophical construct and not one which is concocted from empirical facts. There never was a society in which the members of any class or stratum of people could be characterised in terms of the "wealth of their needs". The individual in ancient society was only apparently such; his wealth was in fact limited. It was the wealth of a man who had not yet cut the umbilical cord of "natural community". Indeed this epoch was characterised by the emergence of man's "human" and "theoretical" senses; it is also true that even in this structure of needs, quality and not quantity predominated. (In *Capital* Marx often underlines — with reference sometimes to Plato and sometimes to Aristotle — the

44

superiority of the thinkers of antiquity in this respect, as compared with the ideologues of the bourgeoisie. He observes ironically how the expropriation which gave birth to the tragic poets and philosophers of Greece ought to be judged differently from that which produced only textile magnates.) However, the community structure that circumscribes unlimited expansion of production not only determines the "limitness" of the versatility of the individual, but also makes the historical period of universality (of rich needs) ephemeral and "reversible" — as in fact it was reversed, in subsequent historical development.

Furthermore, needs are "distributed" qualitatively in the division of labour of those societies based on "natural community". The feudal serf had needs qualitatively different from those of the landed proprietor, not because he could not "acquire" the objects of his needs, but because these were qualitatively different, on the basis of a given nature (in the sense of the natural character of the life of the community). Precisely for this reason, needs had to remain one-sided and limited; they could not become individual, and were all subordinated to the fixed structure of the community. "In general the enjoyment of all *hitherto existing estates and classes* had to be either childish, exhausting or crude, because it was always completely divorced from the vital activity, the real content of the life of the individuals, and more or less reduced to imparting an illusory content to a meaningless activity."[26] The individual "rich in needs", as a socially characteristic type, is therefore a philosophical construct which can only be verified in the future but which, according to Marx, *must* arise in the future: "Neither (objective) nature nor (subjective) nature is directly given a form adequate to the human essence."[27]

We have said that the concept of man "rich in needs", according to Marx's intention, is partly a pure philosophical construct. But he constantly seeks to base it on empirical facts (which also contain a value emphasis). And this is precisely why he makes use of the concept of "human essence".* The human essence (the

---

* The Marxist concept of "human essence" has been intensively analysed by Gyorgy Markus in his study *Marxism and Anthropology*, to which I myself have made frequent reference [see *Hypothese zu einer marxistischen Werttheorie*, Frankfurt, 1969]. Here I only briefly indicate the problem.

wealth of man), of which the conceptual constituents are universality, consciousness, social existence, objective existence and freedom, achieved its characteristic of *Dynamis* when man raised himself to the level of "mankind". What differentiates man as a social being from the animal world are the possibilities of the species in itself. In the course of its process of development, humanity can only realise the possibilities that accord with its given nature as a species. In class societies, this latter quality develops through oppositions. It is on the social plane as a whole that men develop their given qualities in accordance with the species (at least up to a certain point); but human beings as individuals do not participate in the wealth of the social whole. Whilst the individual, subordinated to the division of labour, remains poor (in the broadest sense of the word) there is a parallel enrichment of the species. The highest level of enrichment reached so far, i.e. capitalism, is also the peak of individual impoverishment. The overcoming of alienation (of private property, subsumed under the division of labour) makes every individual able to participate in social wealth as a whole (both as regards enjoyment and as regards activity), and this assumes a new and higher form. Only then will man become a being that accords with the nature of the species for itself, only then will "internal" and "external" nature adequately match the human essence.

A form of alienation that is typical of class society is, according to Marx, religion. In it and in its greatest object, "God", the essential forces of man appear as forces outside of himself that dominate him. Alienation (alienation of the object and of human need) is expressed in religious need. The earthly family gives us the key to the Holy Family. Religious alienation and need will disappear only when humanity has overcome alienation "here on earth". To mere atheism (an attempt to conquer one form of alienation by substituting another for it) one should therefore counterpose communism, the movement which abolishes the discrepancy between the human species and the individual, between essence and being in general, and which thus conquers religious need *as need*. In Marx's interpretation, alienation is not some sort of long-standing "distortion" of the species or of human nature; the essence of man develops within alienation itself, and this creates the possibility for the realisation of man "rich in needs". Marx's exposition becomes passionate in tone when he describes the universalising and enriching aspects of capitalist society. Since the relevant texts are in general well known, we shall only quote a brief passage here:

"The development . . . of the natural sciences to their highest point; likewise the discovery, creation and satisfaction of new needs arising from society itself; the cultivation of all the qualities of the social human being, production of the same in a form as rich as possible in needs, because rich in qualities and relations — production of this being as the most total and universal possible social product . . . is likewise a condition of production founded on capital."[28]

However, capitalism does not only produce new (social) needs and capacities. By generalising the commodity relation, it turns money into the quantitative "embodiment" of social wealth. Needs are no longer allocated, according to their quality, on the basis of the "natural" division of labour; no member of society is excluded in principle from the satisfaction of needs, of whatever quality (one simply has to purchase the objects of one's needs).

At the same time, however, capitalism as a social relation limits the enrichment of needs which is its own creation. According to Marx, it does this in two ways. It reproduces poverty (in particular for the proletariat, for whom it is poverty in the strict sense of the word, and for the bourgeoisie in the philosophical sense of the word); in the last analysis, it limits the development of productive forces (partly because of the law of the falling rate of profit, partly as a result of crises that necessarily recur); and it degrades that highest productive force, the worker.

Very deliberately, Marx emphasises the fact that capitalism creates needs that are "rich and many-sided" at the same time as it impoverishes men and makes the worker a person "without needs". It is here that the theme of "radical needs" appears: this is, as we shall see, more or less the leitmotiv of Marx's "composition". "Man rich in needs" is a philosophically constructed concept; and "the human essence", even though its foundations are empirical, is "only" (and "only" is not to be understood here in a derogatory sense) a value category. However, if the necessity of realising "the essence of the species" and the idea of a future man "rich in needs" originated only in the mind of "a private philosopher or private critic" named Karl Marx, then who would overthrow capitalism, and why? Who would not merely cause it to fall but would also transcend it, in the direction in which Marx envisaged, in spite of the fact that he always rejected the expression "an ideal to be realised"? Theory entering into the masses becomes a material force, but only if the need already exists for them to take it up. When alienation has reached its extreme level, it must produce the need to transcend it, the need for wealth and for the realisation of "the essence of the species". It is the greatest paradox in Marx's theory of alienation, a paradox which, we hope, can express real possibilities.

Following Marx, let us now analyse the alienation of needs in capitalism. We can subdivide the extraordinarily complex set of references into four groups of problems, which we shall examine in turn:

The means/end relation.

Quality and quantity.

Impoverishment (reduction).

Interests.

In alienated development, that is in the alienated "condition" of wealth, every end becomes a means and every means an end. This "inversion" of means and ends is expressed in every aspect of the human essence.

As we have already emphasised, under "normal" (that is, "human") conditions, the main end of man is other man. Alienation changes this main end into means, and man becomes for other man a mere means: a means towards the satisfaction of his own private ends, of his greed.

In all societies labour possesses a dual character: it is abstract labour and concrete labour. The end of concrete labour is to satisfy human needs; the performance of this labour, i.e. work, is itself the means. In alienation (and particularly in capitalism) the end/means relation inherent in labour is turned upside down and becomes its opposite. In commodity producing society, use value (the product of concrete labour) does not serve to satisfy needs. Its essence consists, on the contrary, in satisfying the needs of the person to whom it does not belong. The nature of the use value that the worker produces is all the same to him; he bears no relation to it. It is *abstract labour* which he performs to satisfy his own needs: it is for this reason and this reason alone that he works, to maintain himself, to satisfy his bare "necessary" needs. The process reaches its culmination when, with the machine, the performance of labour becomes mere "means":

"Machine labour preys on the nervous system to an extreme degree, it suppresses the many-sided action of the muscles and takes away all free physical and mental activity. Work itself becomes a means of torture, so that the machine does not free the worker from labour but takes away from him the content of his own labour."[29]

The development of productive forces in a "purely social" society has the "normal" end of lightening the toil of the worker (freeing him from brutal and inhuman forms of labour), of reducing labour time and producing greater wealth for everyone. However, even here the means/end relation is turned upside down. Since in capitalism the production of surplus value is the goal of increased productivity, this latter too becomes a mere means. So the toil of the worker is not lightened, but is rendered more inhumane; working time does not diminish, it increases; and in parallel with the production of wealth, poverty is produced and reproduced (in the literal sense as well as in the philosophical sense).*

According to Marx, the end of social production ought to be the satisfaction of social needs. But capitalist industry and agriculture do not produce for needs, nor for their satisfaction. The end of production is the valorisation of capital, and the satisfaction of needs (on the market) is only a means towards this end.

We witness an "inversion" of the end/means relationship in social and community relations too. In "normal" conditions, the community fulfils an end-function (we shall refer to this later on): togetherness and communal enjoyment are among the highest forms of needs and of satisfaction of need:

---

* For a certain period, following an increase in productivity, working time becomes shorter: from the middle to the end of the nineteenth century there was a shortening of about one third (in the developed capitalist countries). However, it is necessary to note that for almost a hundred years the effective tendency towards the reduction of working time has remained stagnant: on average, it has not fallen below the level of eight hours a day. Today we can even witness a slight increase. In the United States, effective working time oscillates between eight-and-a-half and nine hours!

"Communal activity and communal enjoyment — i.e. activity and enjoyment which are directly expressed and confirmed in real association with other men — will occur wherever such a direct expression of sociability is based on the essence of its content and is adequate to its nature."[30]

When alienation assumes its extreme form (in capitalism) authentic community disappears, because the commodity relation becomes the sole pseudo-"community"; social ends and content (and social togetherness) become means to the private ends of private persons: "only . . . in 'civil society' do the various forms of social connectedness confront the individual as a mere means towards his private purposes, as external necessity."[31] Marx is of the opinion that the communist movement, as a movement, is able to introduce "normality" into the end/means relationship in this respect. The aim of meetings of communist workers is originally propaganda: "But at the same time, as a result of this association, they acquire a new need — the need for society — and what appeared as a means now becomes an end."[32] The need for communal existence (the need for community) becomes the need for an end instead of for a means: in the faces of these workers is reflected "the nobility of man".

Last but not least, the very wealth of needs is converted from an end into a means. "Every person speculates on creating a new need in another . . . each tries to establish over the other an alien power, so as thereby to find satisfaction of his own selfish need."[33] Capitalism is the pimp that by constantly producing new objects creates an unending stream of new needs which make people prostitute themselves. The numerical growth of needs will never be able to become *true* wealth, because it is merely a *means* serving an alienated force, alien to individual human beings, i.e. the expansion of capitalist production: "The extension of products and needs becomes the ingenious and calculating slave of inhuman, artificial and imaginary cravings."[34]

In our present examination of the problem we shall certainly take into consideration the "imaginary" and "ingenious" nature of the "cravings". All the same, "imaginary" needs do not exist. Whether needs are "normal" or whether they are "artificial" (using the word negatively) depends completely upon the value judgements with which we define "normality". However, even if we sought a so-called "objective" criterion we would only be able to conclude that, at any time, "normal" needs are those which individuals deem to be such; "sophisticated" or "unnatural" needs, on the other hand, are those which the majority regards as such.* The concept of "artificial" needs is ambiguous even in Marx. Sometimes he means so-called "luxury needs" which, as has already been pointed out, can only be defined as such in economic terms. (In philosophical terms, they constitute an irrelevant "group of needs".) Elsewhere, they signify the "accumulation" of a specific type of needs, characterised by the fact that the attempt to satisfy them does not guarantee, and indeed may hinder, the development of a qualitatively many-sided, rich world of needs.

If now, in the course of analysing his conception as a whole, we interpret "artificial" or "calculated" needs in this latter sense, it is not going too far to say that Marx actually discovered the problem of "manipulated needs" and indeed of the "manipulation of needs". A given need does not become a "manipulated" need because of its concrete quality, but for the following reasons.

(a) Constantly new objects of needs and hence constantly new needs appear at that point where the production of specific commodities (and of the needs corresponding to them) is most profitable from the point of view of valorising capital.

(b) The true objective is therefore the satisfaction of the needs of an "essentially alien force"; the creation and satisfaction of individual needs, even if this appears to the individual as an end, is in reality only a means in the hands of this "essential force".

(c) The typical consequence of the mechanism of capitalist production is that there is an increase in needs within a group of needs of a determined type, and an orientation of the individual towards their satisfaction — while other types of need, which shape the human personality, which do not help the valorisation of capital and can even hinder it, wither or fail to develop to the same extent. (Thus the expansion of individual consumer goods causes the continuous introduction of new products, and develops such a mass of corresponding needs that it becomes a brake upon the need for free time and a hindrance to its development.)

(d) Individual freedom is therefore mere appearance: the

---

* For more on this subject see my *Hypothese zu einer marxistischen Werttheorie*.

individual chooses the objects of his needs and moulds his personal needs in a way that conforms not with his personality, but with their position in the division of labour.

(e) From one point of view, the individual certainly becomes effectively more rich (he will have more needs and more objects of need), but this enrichment is one-sided and not limited by other needs: since the goal is not the many-sided development of the individual, the individual person becomes the slave of this one-sidedly developed group of needs.

Since Marx made his analysis the situation has changed, but only to a certain extent (the change is significant, but not in relation to our general problem): manipulated needs are not today peculiar only to the dominant classes but affect the majority of the population, at least in the developed capitalist countries. (Today we can see a process of rebellion starting against the manipulation of needs, especially in the United States. It is of the utmost importance that this process should go ahead, together with the "inversion" of the end/means alienation in relation to the community.)

Needs related to the possession of goods can increase infinitely: no other need imposes limits on their growth. Since possession is detached from use and from immediate enjoyment (the role of enjoyment is taken over by possession itself), the increase in needs is quantitative in character. I cannot possess so much as not to want to possess still more: I want "to have" more, even when the concrete qualities of the objects in my possession do not immediately satisfy any kind of need — I become indifferent towards these concrete qualities. What I possess does not "develop" any new, heterogeneous types of need in me, but on the contrary mutilates them. The person who deals in diamonds, as Marx writes, pays no attention to the aesthetic beauty of the diamond, because he sees it only as an embodiment of exchange value. True wealth is, on the contrary, the development of heterogeneous qualities in types of need.

Money, the money relation, is the "inversion" of the "normal" quality-quantity relation; it is the embodiment and the bearer of the quantification of needs. Money is the purely quantitative representation of social wealth:

"The quantity of money becomes to an ever greater degree its sole effective quality. Just as it reduces everything to its abstract form, so it reduces itself in the course of its own movement to quantitative entity. Excess and intemperance come to be its true norm."[35]

The "excess" that arises in the money relation is described in this passage with an unambiguously negative value judgement. We have already noted that Marx's attitude towards capitalism changed between the *Economic and Philosophic Manuscripts of 1844* and the *Grundrisse*. In the *Grundrisse*, pride of place is given to the discovery of the contradictory character of capitalism and, for this reason, the quantification of needs is analysed with a dual value judgement which corresponds to the two opposed constituents of the contradiction. This fact is expressed in Marx by a very significant change in terminology. In the *Manuscripts* the expression "abstract" predominates in his description of the function of money (we may recall that "money has reduced every being to its own *abstraction*!"); in the *Grundrisse* and thereafter this function is, instead, usually indicated by the expression "general". "Reduction to abstract form" always carries in Marx a negative value judgement, whilst the expression "general" always has a positive one. It will be remembered that the reduction of labour to abstract labour (the indifference of the worker for the specific quality of his work in relation both to the product to his labour and to the activity in which he engages) represents the most extreme expression of the alienation of labour, whilst "labour in general", "production in general", "consciousness in general", "industrial activity in general", produce and express wealth in general. Naturally we are talking here merely of a shift in emphasis, not a radical change in outlook. The idea of "generality" as applied to money is also to be found, though in different words, in the *Economic and Philosophic Manuscripts of 1844* ("Money is the alienated ability of mankind"[36]); and conversely, the argument that money relations produce an "abstract" need for enjoyment also appears in the *Grundrisse*, but only once and as a special case ("The abstract search for enjoyment realises that function of money in which it is the material representative of wealth"[37]). The shift in emphasis is, however, beyond doubt.

In the *Grundrisse*, the quantification of needs (as opposed to the system of needs of natural communities) is represented as alienated development and, more precisely, as an alienated but necessary form of development. Both alienation and development are given prominence in the *Economic and Philosophic Manuscripts of 1844*, where they appear as examples of a fichtian ultimate wickedness"; but the main theme is alienation and not development. In the *Grundrisse* the quantification of quality is the overcoming of limitedness; in this work, all the themes of the *Economic and Philosophic Manuscripts* appear, but they are "orchestrated" differently. The quantification of quality is a form of alienation which, in a given historical context, prepares the conditions for the creation of general wealth; there is no other way of attaining such a stage in social development. This kind of "ingenuity" in producing the objects of needs, including those of new ones — the "increase" of needs of one specific type — is represented as *development* and as the necessary condition for such development (and this, too, relates only to one specific historical period):

"When the aim of labour is not a particular product standing in a particular relation to the particular needs of the individual, but money, wealth in its general form, then, firstly, the individual's industriousness knows no bounds; it is indifferent to its particularity, and takes on every form which serves the purpose; it is ingenious in the creation of new objects for a social need, etc. . . . . General industriousness is possible only where every act of labour produces general wealth, not a particular form of it."[38]

However, here too Marx judges capitalism as a society that imposes quantitative limits on quality, and in two different relationships:

"The transformation into money, exchange value as such, as limit of production, [is equivalent to] restriction of the production of use values by exchange value; or that real wealth has to take on a specific form distinct from itself, a form not absolutely identical with it, in order to become an object of production at all."[39]

Let us state explicitly the two relationships mentioned:

1) Value relations limit new objects of need and the creation of new needs within a group of needs. Here we see, as part of the problematic of need, the conception that in capitalist society productivity increases (new use values grow in number and in

54

quality) only so long as surplus value increases. Marx puts forward from time to time the hypothesis of a "point" in capitalist production at which the "production" of new objects of needs and of new needs ceases (the contradiction between the relations of production and the productive forces). We have drawn attention to the fact that, at least until now, Marx's prediction has not been confirmed: the "quantification" of needs does not, in this sense, reduce the quality. But the last passage quoted asserts something else and goes further:

2) Use values that do not represent exchange value cease to be objects of production. Capitalism "quantifies" all its objective expressions and produces them (as it also produces the needs directed towards them) only if it is "profitable" to do so. In this sense Marx often speaks, for example, about the fact that capitalism is hostile to art. Capitalism produces objects of art which are, first and foremost, bearers of exchange value, which yield profit. As far as the average of society is concerned, the needs for high art are stunted in favour of those for a cheap art which is reproduced to an ever greater extent. Capitalism at the same time quantifies the complexly qualitative world of human needs, turns it into quasi-exchange value and renders it "purchasable"; all qualitative needs that can neither be quantified nor purchased are inhibited. This is precisely the reason why in Marx's analysis of money (of pure quantity), in the *Grundrisse*, there appears an apocalyptic world: "These have one mind, and shall give their power and strength unto the beast . . . and that no man might buy or sell, save that he hath the mark or the name of the beast, or the number of his name."[40]

However, money can not only "restrict" quality, quantify qualitative needs and cause those which are not quantifiable to atrophy, it can also quantify the non-quantifiable and transform qualitative needs into their opposite:

"That which is for me through the medium of money — that for which I can pay (i.e. which money can buy) — that am I, the possessor of the money. The extent of the power of money is the extent of my power. Money's properties are my properties and essential powers, the properties and powers of its possessor. Thus, what I am and am capable of is by no means determined by my individuality. . . . Do not I, who thanks to money am capable of all that the human heart longs for, pos-

55

sess all human capacities? Does not my money, therefore, transform all my incapacities into their contrary?"[41]

In the society of the future, in the society that conforms to the species as it really is, the essence of the species will no longer be alienated from man and so will not be able to assume a quantitative form. Human needs and capacities will be of a qualitative nature: the qualitative can be "exchanged" only with the qualitative, and that means exclusively with quality of the *same* kind. (This argument is developed only in the *Economic and Philosophic Manuscripts of 1844*.) The needs of man will then stand in a direct and qualitative relation to the objects of those needs. This is the meaning of the positive overcoming of *private* property and the realisation of the world of *individual* property. ("Individual property" means the direct relation between qualitative needs.)

"Assume man to be man and his relationship to the world to be a human one: then you can exchange love only for love, trust for trust etc. To enjoy art, you must be an artistically cultivated person; to exercise influence over other people, you must be a person with a stimulating and encouraging effect on other people. Every one of your relations to man and to nature must be a specific expression, corresponding to the object of your will, of your real individual life."[42]

Let us repeat once more: in the *Grundrisse* all the themes of the *Economic and Philosophic Manuscripts of 1844* re-emerge, but the value judgement is somewhat different. The "quantification of the unquantifiable" is no less oppressive in the one than in the other; however, by comparison with the *Economic and Philosophic Manuscripts*, the *Grundrisse* underlines the alienated development that is expressed in the quantification of qualitatively restricted needs:

"If money is the general equivalent, if it is purchasing power in general, then everything can be bought, everything can be transformed into money. But it can be transformed into money only insofar as it is alienated. So-called inalienable, eternal possessions . . . thus crumble when money buys them. . . . Everything can be had 'for ready cash'. . . . So just as everything can be alienated for money, so everything can also however be bought for money. Therefore, everything can be appropriated by everyone, and it depends on circumstances what an individual does or does not appropriate for himself and that in turn depends on the money that is in his possession. With it, the individual is in himself lord of all things. . . . There is nothing higher, nothing sacred, etc., from the moment when everything can be possessed by means of money."[43]

The alienation of the essence of the species and the quantification of all the qualities are necessary so that pure qualitative need may come about, even if only as a possibility ("pure qualitative need" meaning not the need *assigned* by the "natural division of labour", but downright *individual* need).

The most significant form of expression of the impoverishment of needs (and of capacities) is the reduction in homogenisation of needs. Both are characteristic of the dominant classes as much as of the working class, but not in the same way.

The need *to have* is that to which all needs are reduced, and which makes them homogeneous. For the dominant classes this "having" is effective possession; it is a need directed towards private property and money in ever increasing *quantity*. The worker's need to have relates instead to mere survival: he lives in order to be able to maintain himself. "All these physical and mental senses have therefore — the sheer estrangement of all these senses — the sense of having."[44] Or again: "All passions and all activity must therefore be submerged in greed. The worker may only have enough for him to want to live, and may only want to live in order to have that."[45] Marx summarises the reduction and homogenisation of needs in capitalism as follows: "The less you are . . . the more you have."* In stating that the worker is a "being without needs", Marx is alluding to this reduction. The worker must be deprived of every need in order to be able to satisfy one need only, that is, the need to keep himself alive. "And you must not only stint the immediate gratification of your senses, as by stinting yourself on food, etc., you must also spare yourself all sharing of general

---

* This is not a new idea. One can find it, formulated in exactly the same way, in Rousseau (*Nouvelle Héloise*) and in Goethe (*Wilhelm Meister*). Since Marx knew these works very well, it is highly probable that he did not get the idea from Hess, even though it is Hess to whom he refers in applying this category.

interest, all sympathy, all trust, etc."[46] There is only one thing which the worker must not be deprived of: his labour power. However, the application of labour power (labour) in capitalist conditions is itself a "process of reduction". The actual carrying out of work does not represent a need as far as the worker is concerned. As a result of the division of labour, "the main force of production"[47] (the main force of production being "the human being himself") is restricted. This concludes the question of the reduction and homogenisation of needs.

Or does it? We have already quoted one of the most important paradoxes in Marx's theory, and we shall return to it: on the one hand, capitalist society reduces to mere "having" and homogenises into "greed" the system of needs both of the dominant class and of the working class (though in different ways); on the other hand, it generates antagonistic "radical needs" which transscend capitalist society, and whose bearers are called upon to overthrow capitalism. According to Marx's formulation in the *Manuscripts*, "The human being had to be reduced to this absolute poverty in order that he might yield his inner wealth to the outer world."[48]

"Interest" is not for Marx a philosophical-social category of a general character. Interest as a motive of individual action is nothing but the expression of the reduction of needs to greed: in the philosophical generalisation of the concept of interest, it is "the standpoint of bourgeois society" that is reflected. The organic moment and the essential feature of the overcoming of alienation is precisely the disappearance of "interest" as a motive. Already in the *Economic and Philosophic Manuscripts of 1844* one can read that "Need or enjoyment have consequently lost their egotistical nature, and nature has lost its mere utility by becoming human use."[49]

However, one observation is necessary here. In contrast to the Marx of the *Manuscripts*, the mature Marx sharply distinguishes the category of "utility" from that of "interest". (In *The Communist Manifesto* it is not utility itself but the reduction to a "usefulness relation" that is equated with the interest relation.)

Let us remind ourselves how Marx describes and explains the concept of use value together with that of utility. From the *Grundrisse* to *Capital*, and finally in the *Marginal Notes to the*

Manual of Political Economy by Adolph Wagner (1881), the concept of utility always appears with a positive value judgement. In the mature works, "utility" and "usefulness" are either simply the qualities of "goods" (when he is employing the naturalistic conception), or they are categories for the orientation of value towards the objects of human activity and enjoyment (when he is employing the non-naturalistic conception). It is only this distinction made in the mature works that is relevant to our problem here. We cannot go deeply into such an analysis here, but let us look briefly at how the concept of utility has developed in the course of the history of philosophy. (I have given a deeper analysis of the useful-harmful pairing of secondary categories of the orientation of value in my *Hypothese zu einer marxistischen Werttheorie*.)

For the ancients, the concept of usefulness played a primary role (e.g. Aristotle: that is good which is useful for man); it continues to be important in medieval thought. Neither ancient nor medieval philosophy knew the category of interest (in my book on Aristotle I wrongly attributed this to the "restrictedness" of ancient society). It is only bourgeois philosophy that has attributed central importance to the categories of interest (individual interest and general interest), an importance that has become proportionately greater as bourgeois society itself has "developed". The "theory of interest" finds its fullest expression in the French Enlightenment and in Hegel. The "theory of utility" in bourgeois philosophy is in truth a "theory of interest": the categories of utility and of interest become synonymous. The critics of capitalism could not get rid of it simply by setting a "citizen" theory of value against the "bourgeois" theory. Marx shows his outstanding genius when with a single move he dispenses not only with the solution but with the whole formulation of the problem. In reply to a letter from Engels arguing that there was a "rational kernel" in Stirner's theory of egoism, Marx expresses in a way that leaves no room for doubt his rejection of such a position, a rejection that we find not only in his critique of Stirner, but later on in the *Grundrisse*. (We may note that this difference between the conceptions of Marx and Engels reappears in the subsequent fate of this category. Engels found it sufficient to substitute for the category of the "individual" interest the general category of the "class interest". Marx, as we shall see, went much further.)

59

As well as rejecting the general-ontological use of the concept of interest, Marx also rejected both the so-called "individual" interest and the general or complexly social categories of interest and all categories used in an analogous way. If at times in *The German Ideology* and even in the *Grundrisse* the controversy is still open, later on Marx expresses his rejection by the fact that he only rarely uses this category. In particular, it is necessary to note that he only very rarely uses the category of class interest. One may search in vain for the concept of "class interest" in works such as the *Grundrisse*, *Capital*, *Wages, Prices and Profit*, or *Theories of Surplus Value*: it does not appear once, not even with reference to the class struggle. The reason for this is not that class interest does not exist for Marx, but because in his view, one was dealing with something that could only be interpreted within the framework of the fetishised reality of capitalism, or, better still, one might say that this concept itself has a fetishistic character. So the "class interest" cannot be the motive of a class struggle that goes beyond capitalist society: the true motive, free from fetishism, is represented by the "radical needs" of the working class. It was Engels (in *Anti-Dühring*) who pointed to class interest as one of the factors determining the class struggle: to be precise, however, we ought to note that for Engels it was not one of those exclusive and unequivocal terms which come into common use in later marxist analysis (from the time of the Second International, particularly in Kautsky).

In Marx, the duality between individual interests and "general" or "class interests" is nothing but the expression of the fact that, from the point of view of motivation, man in bourgeois society is split into "bourgeois" and "citizen". The individual interest is the (openly recognised) motive of the bourgeois, while it is the general interest which motivates the citizen. Both are alienated motivations; but in the latter there is a double alienation, since here the "individual interest" is alienated also from the individual himself.

Let us now consider the most important passage in which these categories are dealt with. In *The Holy Family*, dealing with "the declaration of the rights of man", Marx writes as follows:

"As the state of old had slavery as its natural basis, the modern state has civil society and the man of civil society, i.e. the independent man depending on other men only by

60

private interest and unconscious natural necessity, the slave of earning his living and of his own as well as other men's selfish need. The modern state has recognised this as its natural basis in the universal rights of man."[50]

In this quotation, an idea from the *Economic and Philosophic Manuscripts of 1844* reappears, this time with a specific reference. "Private interest" is simply the so-called greed that is a consequence of the "reduction" of needs. It is no accident that expressions such as "natural necessity", the "natural basis", or "slave", play such a decisive role. They are not mere relics of a sort of "feuerbachism"; the question in all its interconnections is and remains central to the thought of Marx. Civil society, the first "pure society", functions in fact in its pure social relations as "quasi-nature", because in it, necessity reigns in the form of economic chains. Man, having become the "slave" of his own private interests, of his own egoism and of others, is a quasi-natural being, because his egoism is of a compulsive character and functions as a quasi-instinct: man must follow its dictates or end in ruin. "Therefore, it is natural necessity, essential human properties, however alienated they may seem to be, and interest that hold the members of civil society together, civil, not political life is their real tie."[51]

In *The German Ideology* (in the attack on Stirner), Marx gives a highly coherent treatment of the double alienation of the "general interest" (and of the "class interest"). Let us quote the most important passages in full.

"How is it that personal interests always develop, against the will of individuals, into class interests, into common interests which acquire an independent existence in relation to the individual persons, and in this independent existence assume the form of general interests? How is it that as such they come into contradiction with actual individuals and in this contradiction, by which they are defined as general interests, they can be conceived by consciousness as ideal and even as religious, holy interests? *How is it that in this process of private interests acquiring independent existence as class interests the personal behaviour of the individual is bound to be rendered banal, to be alienated,* and at the same time exists as a power independent of him and without him, created by intercourse, and becomes transformed into social relations, into a series of powers which determine and subordinate the individual, and which, therefore, appear in the imagination as 'holy' powers? If Sancho had only understood the fact that within the framework of certain modes of production (which are, of course, independent of the will) there are alien practical forces above men, which are independent not only of isolated individuals but also of their totality . . . [Stirner] would not then have arrived at the absurdity — worthy of him — of explaining the division between personal and general interests by saying that people represent this division to themselves in a religious way too, and that they match each other in this or that way, which is, however, only another word for 'representation'."[52]

The principal observations that we can dig out from this and other passages are as follows.

(a) The "general" interest and the "class" interest do not exist only as man's representations, as an ideal pole opposed to their own personal interests. They are categories of social structures governed by social forces that are independent of men and assert themselves against the will of the individual. The existence of "general interests" therefore mirrors the fetishisation of social relations (this process culminates in a society that is purely a "producer of commodities", that is, in capitalism).

(b) The personal interest and the general or class interest are correlated.

(c) Whatever "interest" is chosen — be it theoretical or practical — one remains within the commodity producing (capitalist) society, that is, its fetishistic character is accepted.

"Communists do not put egoism against self-sacrifice or self-sacrifice against egoism. . . . Communist theoreticians, the only ones who have time to devote to the study of history, are distinguished precisely because they alone have discovered that throughout history the 'general interest' is created by individuals who are defined as 'private persons'. They know that this contradiction is only a seeming one because one side of it, the so-called 'general', is constantly being produced by the other side, private interest, and by no means opposes the latter as an independent force with an independent history — so that this contradiction is in practice always being destroyed and reproduced."[53]

This quotation bears witness to the fact that communists do

not refer to any kind of "general interest", not even to class interest. They cannot consider it a motive for class struggle transcending capitalism, because to refer to it means, by that very fact, to *remain within the capitalist world*. Reference to working-class interests is therefore possible only in class struggle that does not transcend capitalism: then, in fact, it is realistic, because it invokes a category of Being (the fetishistic correlation of personal interests). One should not therefore be surprised that at the time of the Second International the reference to class interest (in no way corresponding to the spirit of Marx) should have been so widespread. Every movement that is limited to a programme adequate to the egoistical interests of the individual worker (above all the struggle for wages, which opens up for each worker the prospect of a greater material wealth in the narrow sense), realistically and with reason, invokes the "class interest".

It is questionable whether Marx changed this position in his later works or not. As we have indicated, in his scientific works reference is only rarely made to the category of the "general" and "common" interest, or to the concept of the "class interest". We shall look at the passages in question and analyse their meaning.

In the *Grundrisse* (in the analysis of commodity exchange), he says:

"The reciprocity in which each is at the same time means and end and attains his end only insofar as he becomes a means, and becomes a means only insofar as he posits himself as end, that each thus posits himself as being for another, insofar as he is being for self, and the other as being for him, insofar as he is being for himself — that this reciprocity is a necessary fact presupposed as natural precondition of exchange, but that, as such, it is irrelevant to each of the two subjects in exchange, and that this reciprocity interests him only insofar as it satisfies his interest to the exclusion of it, without reference to that of the other. That is, the common interest which appears as the motive of the act as a whole is recognised as a fact by both sides; but, as such, it is not the motive, but rather proceeds, as it were, behind the back of these self-reflected particular interests, behind the back of one individual's interest in opposition to that of the other."[54] (The reasoning demonstrates that the various forms of alienation of needs are only different

63

aspects of an identical process, although they are here treated separately for the purpose of greater clarity. In this passage Marx treats the alienation of interests — the interest relation — as a form of end/means alienation.)

Marx concludes: "The general interest is precisely the generality of self-seeking interests."

If there is a difference between the arguments in *The German Ideology* and this passage from the *Grundrisse*, it does not relate to the essence of the problem discussed here. It consists rather in the broader scope with which the problem is raised in *The German Ideology*; there, it is a question of the different *forms* of the "general interest", and of the forms in which the "general interest" can serve as the *motive*, albeit an alienated one (it is this, for example, that motivates man as citizen). This work deals not only with economic interests (as general interests) but also with "generalised interests" of every kind (political interests, state interests and so forth). Since it is commodity exchange that is being discussed in the passages from the *Grundrisse*, the analysis of the "general interest" must obviously be restricted there to economic interest.

But from our point of view such a distinction is irrelevant. In the *Grundrisse* too, the "general interest" is represented as doubly alienated interest. The world of commodity exchange is the world of the universality of egoism: that of personal interest. The subjects of exchange are indifferent to each other; they stand in relation to each other only for the realisation of their personal interests: as regards the "need for other people" (which, as we know, Marx considered to be the highest and "most human" need), the reduction is total. "General interests" assert themselves behind the backs of men who have already been reduced to selfishness. In this sense, therefore, the general interest is simply the *restriction* of one human being's interests by those of another: a structure that Hegel in his *Phenomenology of Mind* defines as "the animal realm of the spirit". In this sense, the "general interest" is an alienated power resulting from the struggle between private interests, and thwarting the ends and aims of individual human beings. Referring to this in *The German Ideology*, Marx describes it as the determining power of *all* the alienated "general interests", and therefore as the key to those interests that motivate human beings.

We come now to the crucial concept of the "class interest". In *Wage Labour and Capital* there are two passages which Marx himself underlines:

"To say that the interests of capital and those of the workers are one and the same is only to say that capital and wage labour are two sides of one and the same relationship. The one determines the other, as usurer and squanderer reciprocally condition the existence of each other."

And later on:

"We see, therefore, that even if we remain within the relationship of capital and wage labour, the interests of capital and the interests of wage labour are diametrically opposed."[55]

Here, the problem is raised chiefly from the point of view of the struggle for wages, a form of class struggle that can be interpreted only within capitalist society. ("Even if we remain within the relationship of capital and wage labour" is therefore a superfluous qualification, because according to Marx the struggle for wages is only conceivable within the relationship between wage labour and capital.) The relations on the basis of which the struggle between "wage labour" and "capital" takes place are fetishistic relations, within which the use of the category "interests" (which, as we know, is an objective category) can be interpreted in a completely rational way, in accordance with the concept of "class interests" in *The German Ideology*. It should be added that the concept can be rationally interpreted only in this sense. Furthermore, Marx did not speak of "the interests of the working class", but of the interests of wage labour: of interests that derive from the reality of exploitation and, moreover, from the reality of a specific form of exploitation. In such a context the working class is reduced to its immediate relationship with capital, in which capital and wage labour are "two sides of one and the same relationship". It is therefore a reciprocal determination [*Reflexionbestimmung*]. Here he is not talking about a working class which transcends capitalism (nor could he), and still less is he talking about the "radical needs", which cannot be reduced to "interests".

Not once is this very restricted interpretation of the concept of interest to be found in *Wages, Prices and Profit*, a much later work in which partly analogous problems are dealt with. This is no accident. At the centre of Marx's analysis in this work stands a critique of the "reduction" of the trade union struggle to a struggle for wages. The difference is not quantitative in nature but qualitative. The wages struggle which, as we have seen, remains "within" capitalism, "within" the "system of interests", is qualitatively different from the struggle to overcome the wages system as a whole, which is the historical mission of the working class, motivated not by interest but by the "radical needs".

"Trades unions work well as centres of resistance against the encroachments of capital. . . . *They fail generally from limiting themselves* to a guerrilla war against the effects of the existing system, instead of simultaneously trying to change it, instead of using their organised forces as a lever for the *final emancipation of the working class, that is to say, the ultimate abolition of the wages system.*"[56]

III

The Concept of "Social Need"

In Marx's view, the concept of "social need" is not a category which is in itself alienated, but one which has a rational meaning in every society, even after the positive overcoming of alienation. However, it is one of his least precise concepts, and he uses it in several different ways. It is used to describe various social facts including, often, the capitalist alienation of needs: but if we study the main tendency of Marx's thought we shall find that this interpretation is only one amongst many, and that it is only relevant for capitalist society. It is therefore completely foreign to his overall conception to identify the category of "the general interest" with that of "social need". This point must be strongly emphasised, because in marxist writing the two categories are commonly treated as synonymous. I am referring not only to the fetishistic interpretation of the concept of "social need", but also to the assumption of positive value which lies behind this fetishised interpretation. It is formulated in such a way that "social need" becomes a "need of society": not the whole or the average of the personal needs of individuals, nor the evolving tendency of such needs, nor "socialised" personal need, but a *general* system of needs which, so to speak, is "suspended above" individual people and is at a higher level than the personal needs of the individuals who constitute society. This conception has led to various conclusions (and consequences) both in theory and in practice. The two most important of these should be mentioned.

(a) Since the so-called "social need" is more general and at a higher level than "personal" need, then in cases of conflict the individual should subordinate to the "social need" his own demands for satisfaction of his personal needs. In practice, this kind of "social need" turns out to be the need of the privileged or dominant layers of the working class (or of society), disguised by their halo of "general validity".

(b) "Social needs" are the real, "genuine" needs of individual people; those people who have *de facto* needs which cannot be represented as "social need" simply have "not yet recognised" their "genuine" needs. From this conception there follows a distinction between "recognised" and "unrecognised" needs. But who is to decide which of people's needs are genuine? Once again, it can only be the representatives of the so-called "social need". In other words, the actual needs of the privileged and of the leaders of the movement are incarnations of "universality" and "socialisation", and it is they who decide which of the needs of the class (that is, of the overwhelming majority of the population) are "correct" and which "incorrect": thus the actual, existing needs of the majority are classified as "false". The "representatives" of the "social needs" then take it upon themselves to decide the needs of the majority, and to pursue the alleged "unrecognised needs" instead of people's real and actual needs.

I shall leave aside the practical consequences of this fetishisation of the concept of social needs, and simply add that the fetishised concept of need has been "fabricated" in a similar way to that of interest. We have already seen, on the basis of Marx's own analysis, that the subordination of self to the "general" interest is in fact correlated with the pursuit of personal interest. (Both the "bourgeois" and the "citizen" are necessary to the functioning of bourgeois society.) Moreover, we can sensibly distinguish between "recognised" and "unrecognised" interests. Interest is in fact constituted by opposition of interests (the identity of interests is really the identity of their opposition). Interest is the reduction and at the same time the homogenisation of needs, in the same way that we give to Self (whether "Self" signifies a person, an association or a class) the value of our own "reciprocal determination" *against* others: it is therefore realistic to assert that the person (the nation, the class etc.) who fails to assert himself over others is failing to act in accordance with his own interests. Furthermore, if a person (an association, a class) does not clearly see the optimal means of asserting his claims, then he has "not recognised" his "own interests". If the optimal means of asserting claims in the intercourse of the various objectivations are different or directly opposed, one may then reasonably speak of "conflicts of interest".

Let us return to Marx's position. As we have seen, he speaks on various occasions of "real" and "imaginary" needs, but never and nowhere does he speak of "unconscious" or "unrecognised" needs (both the "real" and the "imaginary" are conscious). Moreover, it is precisely in order to circumvent the category of "unrecognised" needs that Marx requires the concept of "radical needs" (he ascribes the latter to the working class more than once, though he does not consider them as being present *de facto* in the class). Where there are "unrecognised needs" there are also "educators", whose job it is to make people "conscious" of their needs. But it is well known that Marx rejected this conception of "unrecognised needs" as early as the *Theses on Feuerbach* (where he treats it as what it really is: a category from the Enlightenment).

Marx recognises no needs other than those of individual people. One may calculate or budget for an average of individual needs (as we have seen in the case of "necessary needs"), but these are still the needs of individual people. Only in his description of fetishism does Marx use the category of need with its fetishistic meaning (in order to contrast it with needs which are not fetishistic and which are therefore those of individuals). Let us take, for example, the passages from *Capital* quoted on page (24), where he defines capitalist alienation by the fact that it is not the worker's needs of development that are decisive but "the need to valorise capital". This latter expression is consciously used here in a fetishistic sense. For although the need to valorise capital is always the need of an individual capitalist, the capitalist too is an alienated power, a representative of capital. In capitalist society, relationships between human beings (like needs) appear as reified relationships — but in fact they are still relationships between human beings.

As I have already said, Marx uses the concept of "social needs" in various senses. The most important meaning (and the most frequently used) is that of "socially produced" need. The relevant passages have already been quoted in the first chapter, and I will not repeat them here. "Socially produced" needs are the needs of *individual human beings*. In some places this classification includes, as a whole, needs "that are not natural needs", and in other places it includes all needs indiscriminately. In this latter interpretation, "socially produced" need is synonymous with human need, where "human" is *not* a value category.

In another sense that appears less often, but nevertheless with a certain frequency, "social need" is a positive value category: it is the need of man for communism, the need of the so-called "socialised man". In the third volume of *Capital*, capitalist society is once again contrasted with the society of associated producers, precisely from the standpoint of needs:

"The expansion or contraction of production are determined by . . . profit and the proportion of this profit to the employed capital, thus by a definite rate of profit, *rather than the relation of production to social needs, i.e. to the needs of socially developed human beings.*"[57]

Here, therefore, "social need" means the needs of "socially developed humanity". It is unnecessary to emphasise that here too "social need" means the need of the individual human being.

"Social need" is given a third meaning when it is used to describe average needs for material goods in a society or a class. When Marx uses the concept in this sense, he often puts the expression "social need" in inverted commas, and he does so deliberately. "Social need" in inverted commas is the expression of needs in the form of effective demand; without the inverted commas it means those needs (relating to material goods) which do not find expression in effective demand. The distinction is only relevant for Marx in relation to the working class, since he admits that for the ruling classes material need and effective demand at least overlap; and, generally speaking, effective demand is greater than the real need (the "necessary need") of the ruling classes. For the working class, the discrepancy lies between "social need", which appears in the form of effective demand, and so-called "true" social need, the latter not only quantitatively outstripping the former but also containing qualitatively concrete needs of a different kind. In *Capital*, Marx says:

" 'Social need', i.e. the factor which regulates the principle of demand, is essentially subject to the mutual relationship of the different classes and their respective economic position."[58]

A few pages later, arguing the matter more deeply, he says:

"It would seem, then, that there is on the side of demand a certain magnitude of definite social needs which require for their satisfaction a definite quantity of a commodity on the market. But the quantitative determination of this need is very elastic and changing. Its fixedness is only apparent. If the means of subsistence were cheaper, or money wages higher, the labourers would buy more of them, and a greater 'social need' would arise for them. . . . The limits within which the need for commodities represented on the market (i.e. demand) is quantitatively different from *real social need* naturally vary considerably from one commodity to another."[59]

"Social need" here refers to demand and is therefore mere *appearance* which does not express the "real" social needs of the working class, and so disguises them as their opposite.

But what are these real social needs? For Marx, the content of this category corresponds essentially to the empirical and sociological content of *necessary* needs. It needs to be emphasised, however, that this is an average; more precisely, it is the average of individual needs (historically developed, handed down by custom and containing moral aspects). We are dealing here with an objective category: a given human being, belonging to a given class, at a given period of time, is born into a system and hierarchy of needs which, although it is determined by the objects of his needs and by the customs and morality of preceding generations, is nevertheless constantly changing; he will internalise this, even though in an individual manner (to a greater or lesser extent in different societies).

This is in no way, however, an autonomous structure, "suspended above" the members of a class or of a society. The need of the individual is what he knows and feels to be his need — he has no other needs. Thus in the *Economic and Philosophic Manuscripts of 1844* Marx laments "the absence of needs" amongst the workers. He is not saying that workers are conscious of the needs which appear in the form of effective demand but unconscious of their "true" needs that do not appear in this form; "in the latter case, social needs would not be 'flexible' ". What he is saying is rather that true social needs represent actual, thoroughly conscious needs, whilst the "social needs" that are presented on the market indicate the possibilities of satisfying true social needs in a given society. It is not a question of a contrast between conscious and unconscious, but, as Marx says in *The Poverty of Philosophy*, of a contrast between being and not being, between realising and not realising, between what is satisfiable and what is not satisfiable.

Let us add that Marx applies this interpretation of social needs

71

only to material needs, and to those non-material needs that are purchasable by means of exchange value. As regards other non-material needs, the category of "social need" in the above sense is altogether irrelevant. It is, of course, true that there is an objective character not only to material needs, that is to "social needs" as interpreted above, but also to needs generically: to the need for artistic activity, or the need for fellowship or love. (The system of needs already realised, i.e. the hierarchy of needs, "guides" the needs of man born in a specific society, because needs can only develop in interaction with objects and realisations as objects, and because these "objects" demarcate the limits of the needs.) But Marx *never* considers the need for artistic activity or love as "social needs" in the sense specified here. The satisfaction of such needs through exchange value is for him, as we have already seen, the most characteristic form of the phenomenon of alienation: the quantification of the unquantifiable.

Let us look finally at the fourth meaning of social needs: the social (or sometimes: "communal") satisfaction of needs. This is a non-economic interpretation, serving to define or express the fact that men have needs which are not only socially produced, but which, also, are satisfiable only by the creation of corresponding social institutions. In modern society, for example, the satisfaction of the need to learn is possible only by means of adequate institutions for public instruction. The same thing applies to the need for health care and to innumerable kinds of cultural need, even to the need for community. (In this last case the creation of appropriate institutions is not absolutely necessary. However, it is a need which, by its very nature, is satisfiable only in togetherness with others.)

Although the category is not economic, we can however find an economic aspect in it. In the *Critique of the Gotha Programme*, Marx writes that it is necessary to deduct from the gross income of labour "that which is destined for the communal satisfaction of needs such as schools, health services, etc."[60] It is interesting to observe how Marx attributes to purely material "social needs" a character of relative quantitative stability (their quantity should increase almost exclusively in parallel with growth of the population). The part of these social values that serves the "communal satisfaction of needs" will increase rapidly in the future (an ever greater percentage of the gross income of labour will be necessary for the satisfaction of such needs): "From the outset this part is considerably increased in comparison with present day society and it increases in proportion as the new society develops."[61] Needless to say, Marx most certainly does not consider this shift as the "true", "conscious" needs of men becoming related to personal consumption, with "unrecognised" needs becoming represented by the "communal satisfaction of needs". For the future, Marx envisages men for whom, *ab ovo*, these needs (which are only satisfiable socially) appear as *conscious* and *personal* needs, the satisfaction of which will be so important that they themselves will set the limit on other needs. We know that, according to Marx, in the society of associated producers it is only other needs which set limits on human needs. When the domination of things over human beings ceases, when relations between human beings no longer appear as relations between things, then *every* need governs "the need for the development of the individual", the need for the self-realisation of the human personality.

IV

"Radical Needs"

Marx always attributes positive values to communism and constantly contrasts them with the alienated character of past values, those of "pre-history" and particularly those of capitalism. This attribution of value by Marx is characterised, subjectively, by "Ought" [*das Sollen*]: communism *should* be realised. But from the very beginning Marx is also forced to surmount this Ought (the subjectivity of Ought) theoretically. He finds two ways of doing this; they are not always differentiated, but they can be. The first is the transformation of the *subject* into the *collectivity*. The Ought itself is *collective*, because at the maximum point of capitalist alienation it stimulates certain needs among the masses (and particularly among the proletariat); these are the radical needs which embody this Ought and which, by their very nature, tend to transcend capitalism — and precisely in the direction of communism. The second way is the transformation of Ought into *causal necessity*. "Communism should be realised" is, in this case, a principle synonymous with the idea that it will necessarily be realised by the inherent laws of the economy. It might be said that sometimes it is a fichtian conception which prevails in Marx, and sometimes a hegelian one (both, of course, are "inverted").

This fluctuating attitude is expressed, *inter alia*, when Marx oscillates between a conception of economic laws as "laws of nature" and the contrary conception. In the well known preface of 1867 to the first volume of *Capital*, he writes of his standpoint as one from which "the evolution of the economic formation of society is viewed as a process of natural history."[82] It only needs to be added that in the postscript to the second edition (1873) he draws our attention to his conscious use of the hegelian method. Not so well known are the observations that contradict this position. In the third volume of *Theories of Surplus Value* Marx writes that when capitalism comes to be analysed historically, "the illusion of regarding (the economic

74

laws of a social formation) as natural laws of production vanishes".[63] And even in the first volume of *Capital* he speaks of a "law of capitalist accumulation, metamorphosed by economists into a pretended law of nature".[64] It might be objected that "the process of natural history" and "law of nature" are not synonymous. But the objection is not valid, because in the preface that has been quoted one can already read, in so many words, the expression "law of nature", in a context which is for us particularly important, the context of the historical perspective:

> "And even when a society has got on to the right track for the discovery of the natural laws of its movement . . . it can neither clear by bold leaps, nor remove by legal enactments, the obstacles offered by the successive phases of its normal development. But it can shorten and lessen the birth pangs."[65]

We shall see that there is an analagous interpretation for the "negation of the negation".

In his letter to the editors of *Otecestvennye Zapiski* Marx again raises doubts about the naturalistic interpretation. And in his rough notes for a letter replying to Vera Zasulic, he writes about the possibility of reaching communism by a circuitous route, "jumping over" capitalism. (Thus there also exists the possibility of "jumping" some "stages of development".) Primitive accumulation is not therefore a "general law", and the proletarianisation of the peasantry is not a "necessity". Indeed, Marx writes with a tone of resignation: "If Russia continues to tread the path on which it has travelled since 1861, it will *lose the finest opportunity* that history has ever offered a people, and will experience all the inevitably circuitous journeyings through the régime of capitalism."[66] As so often when he is examining concrete historical problems, Marx substitutes the concept of "alternatives" for that of "necessity".

In the other conception, however, the category of "Possibility" occupies as small a position as it does in the hegelian conception of "economic law". In order to understand this and the central problem of "radical needs", we must briefly consider Marx's conception of "the social totality".

Every social formation is a total Whole, a unity of structures coherently linked to each other and constructed interdependently. There is no causal relationship between these structures (no one of them is the "cause" or the "consequence" of another); they are only able to function as parts of an interdependent arrangement. In *The Poverty of Philosophy* Marx formulates this as follows:

"The production relations of every society form a whole. M. Proudhon considers economic relations as so many social phases, engendering one another, resulting one from the other like the antithesis from the thesis, and realising in their logical sequence the impersonal reason of humanity. . . . How, indeed, could the single logical formula of movement, of sequence, of time, explain the structure of society, in which *all relations coexist simultaneously and support one another?*"[87]

In the *Introduction to a Critique of Political Economy*, explaining the problems of production, exchange and consumption, Marx concludes: "The conclusion we reach is not that production, distribution, exchange and consumption are identical, but that they all form the members of a totality, distinctions within a unity."[88] And in the *Grundrisse* he says, "Forces of production and social relations (are) two different sides of the development of the social individual."[69] Also, in the well known passage in which he deals in detail with the relation between the economic base and ideological forms, Marx concerns himself with the reciprocal composition of these structures. The life processes of society manifest themselves in the superstructure, since the moments of the latter "bring out" [*austragen*] the conflicts of the base.

Now from our point of view, why is the conception of the social totality (the "formation") important? It is because this conception makes it possible to locate the foundations of the collective Ought in Being. For the present, let us briefly say that one of the essential interdependent structures of capitalism as "formation" is the structure of need. To be able to function in the form characteristic of Marx's epoch, to be able to subsist as "social formation", capitalism had to have, within its structure of need, certain needs that were not satisfiable internally. According to Marx, radical needs are *inherent* aspects of the capitalist structure of need: without them, as we have said, capitalism cannot function, so it creates them afresh every day. "Radical needs" cannot be "eliminated" from capitalism because they are necessary to its functioning. They are not the "embryos"

76

of a future formation, but "members" of the capitalist formation: it is not the *Being* of radical needs that transcends capitalism but their *satisfaction*. Those individuals for whom the "radical needs" already arise in capitalism are the bearers of the "collective Ought".

In order to deepen the discussion of this problem it is, however, also necessary to analyse the antinomies of capitalism.

Naturally the two kinds of "transformation" of Ought, which we have traced back to Fichte and Hegel respectively, also find expression in the theory of the antinomies of capitalism: "naturally", because the problem of what are the opposites to be surmounted and the problem of how to surmount them are organically connected.

We begin with the "hegelian" conception of antinomy, which is better known and also easier. Let us refer to two unambiguous passages, one from the *Preface to the "Critique of Political Economy"*, the other from the first volume of *Capital*. (Analagous formulations are to be found in the *Communist Manifesto* and in passages of *Anti-Dühring* in which Engels explains Marx's conception.)

In the *Preface* he writes:

"At a certain stage of development, the material productive forces of society come into conflict with the existing relations of production or — this merely expresses the same thing in legal terms — with the property relations within the framework of which they have operated hitherto. From forms of development of the productive forces these relations turn into their fetters."[70]

Marx explains a general law here, which is valid for *every* social formation (though elsewhere he is opposed to the formulation of social laws of universal validity).

In every social formation, relations of production are first established which correspond to the level of development of the productive forces, and which for a certain period contribute to the development of the productive forces. But subsequently oppositions develop that lead to contradiction, whereby the relations of production become fetters on the productive forces. Here the point is to invert the hegelian conception of contradiction and thus to change it. The course of development (of the forces and relations of production) in every social formation would accordingly be correspondence — opposition — contradiction.

In the first book of *Capital*, in the chapter on "The Historical Tendency of Capitalist Accumulation", Marx shows how capitalism developed the productive forces and how, in parallel, the oppositions within this society have unfolded. He concludes as follows:

"The monopoly of capital becomes a fetter upon the mode of production, which has sprung up and flourished along with, and under it. Centralisation of the means of production and socialisation of labour at last reach a point where they become incompatible with their capitalist integument. This integument is burst asunder. The knell of capitalist private property sounds. The expropriators are expropriated.

The capitalist mode of appropriation, the result of the capitalist mode of production, produces capitalist private property. This is the first negation of individual private property, as founded on the labour of the proprietor. But capitalist production begets, with the inexorability of a law of Nature, its own negation. It is the negation of negation. This does not re-establish private property for the producer, but gives him individual property based on the acquisitions of the capitalist era: i.e. on co-operation and the possession in common of the land and of the means of production produced by labour itself."[71]

This passage describes the phases of capitalist development as follows. For a certain period capitalism develops the productive forces to an extraordinary degree, through the socialisation of production. Then the socialised productive forces and the relations of production enter into contradiction. This contradiction sharpens, becomes irreconcilable and finally reaches the "point" at which the centralisation of the means of production breaks the "shell" of capitalism. The capitalist mode of production brings about its own negation with the necessity of a natural process. Of course capitalism does not collapse of its own accord: it is overturned by the proletariat. But this overturning is necessary because of capitalism's economic dysfunction. Quite rightly Marx denies having simply adapted the hegelian model to his own way of thinking, and asserts that he is using it only to express his own conceptions. We have seen that this assertion is valid. In fact

Marx's theory of contradiction can be traced back to Hegel simply in the sense that the hegelian formula is an *adequate* mode of expression for it.

But what is the role of "radical needs" in this conception? In the context which I have already quoted Marx writes, with reference to these needs:

"Along with the constantly diminishing number of the magnates of capital . . . grows the mass of misery, oppression, slavery, degradation, exploitation; but with it too grows the revolt of the working class, a class always increasing in numbers, and disciplined, united, organised by the very mechanism of the process of capitalist production itself."[72]

However one reads this passage, the theory of absolute impoverishment is clearly formulated (poverty *grows* with the development of capitalism). At the same time the theme of "radical needs" also emerges. We are thus confronted with the most paradoxical possible articulation of the paradox to which we have referred. If the negation of the negation were a natural law, no kind of radical need whatever would be necessary for the downfall of capitalism.

These passages from *Capital* clearly demonstrate that Marx, in the hegelian sense, "objectivised" Ought in social necessity, or rather in economic necessity, thus removing precisely its character as "Ought". The generalisation of the hegelian theory of contradiction into a global social law is, of course, only a consequence of this. The fact that the contradiction between the productive forces and the relations of production (where the latter are smashed by the development of the former) appears in *every* society is the historical demonstration of the necessity for capitalism to collapse. It should be added that Marx here is ruthlessly consistent — more so than Engels — about there always being another possibility, i.e. the ruin of the productive forces (since the *Manifesto* is a jointly written work we cannot refer to it in this connection):

"The capitalist mode of production more and more completely transforms the great majority of the population into proletarians, it creates the power which, under penalty of its own destruction, is forced to accomplish this revolution."[73]

The fact that Engels poses the alternative here is without a doubt a merit on his part, but there is still a certain one-sidedness in his conception. Of Marx's two theories of contradiction Engels in fact accepts only one exclusively (the hegelian version); hence this is the only one in which he can "find room" for practice. But Marx had an additional, fundamentally different theory of contradiction which is of no less significance.

This second conception of contradiction cannot be generalised with reference to past history: Marx himself several times underlines the point that it cannot be generalised (for example in the first volume of *Capital*, in the chapter on commodity fetishism). According to this conception, the antinomies that are expressed in capitalism are the contradictions of advanced commodity production. And the structure of the first part of the first volume of *Capital* (commodities - money - capital) is founded upon the unfolding of precisely these antinomies. The commodity is use value and exchange value; from the very beginning (from the moment at which products are turned into commodities), these develop oppositions of a contradictory character. The commodity is not the unity of opposites but the form in which the opposites move. The commodity form is the embryo of the antinomies of capitalism, and these contradictions are already contained in the embryo itself.

In the production of commodities, human relations assume the form of relations between things; social existence becomes fetishised in "the thing" [*zu Dinglichem fetischisiert*]. Social relations fetishised in "the thing" confront individual human beings in the form of economic laws — laws of nature, as it were. The functioning of social power is mystified into a law of nature:

"All the different kinds of private labour, which are carried on independently of each other, and yet as spontaneously developed branches of the social division of labour, are continually being reduced to the quantitative proportions in which society requires them. And why? Because in the midst of all the accidental and ever fluctuating exchange-relations between the products, the labour-time socially necessary for their production forcibly asserts itself like an over-riding law of Nature."[74]

However, this mystified expression of economic laws in the form of natural laws is precisely and exclusively the consequence of commodity production, its inner essence:

"The value-form of the product of labour is not only the *most abstract*, but is also the *most universal* form, taken by the product in the bourgeois mode of production . . . If then we treat this mode of production as one eternally fixed by Nature for every state of society, we necessarily overlook the specificity of the value form, and consequently of the commodity-form, and of its further developments, money-form, capital-form, etc."[75]

These are the forms which "bear it stamped upon them in unmistakeable letters that they belong to a state of society, in which *the process of production has the mastery over man, instead of being controlled by him.*"[76]

Before starting to analyse the antinomies of commodity production I want to emphasise the fact that this conception logically contradicts any statement that the realisation of the society of associated producers is a law of nature. The functioning of the economy in the guise of natural law belongs in fact to commodity production and only to it, as an expression of commodity fetishism. The positive overcoming of private property cannot. therefore in any way proceed in the form of a "natural necessity"; the essence of this process is the overcoming of fetishism and the revolutionary liquidation of the appearance which social existence has of being a quasi-law of nature. Although it has economic aspects, the transition *cannot* be a purely economic process, but must be a total social revolution and is only conceivable as such.

For Marx the specific antinomies of capitalism, which derive from commodity production, are those between *freedom and necessity, necessity and chance, teleology and causality;* from these follows the special antinomy of social wealth and social impoverishment. These are the antinomies of the "pure" society in which economic development assumes the status of natural law and in which — to recall *Capital* once again — man is subordinated to the process of production and not the process of production to man.

First let us consider the antinomy of freedom and necessity. In commodity production the producer is a free man, a man who has cut "the umbilical cord of the natural community": commodity exchange itself is an act of freedom and equality. Every producer of commodities freely pursues his own private interest (we refer once again to the passage in Marx) if, when he exchanges his commodity, he exchanges "like for like". Marx says the same thing about wage labour. The wage labourer is free;

without free labour power, capitalist accumulation could never have started (one of the functions of primitive accumulation was that of bringing free labour power on to the market). However, the free commodity producer and the free labourer are equally subordinated to the quasi-natural necessity of the economy, which asserts itself behind the backs of the "free" actions of individual human beings.

This antagonism is part of the essence of commodity production, i.e. of capitalism, from the first moment of its appearance.

Let us look briefly at the antinomy of necessity and chance. Marx associates the law of value (according to which value is defined by the socially necessary labour time) not exclusively with capitalism but with every society in which the sphere of production is rational; the law of value therefore will assume its most pure form in the society of "associated producers". In the third volume of *Capital*, Marx writes:

"This reduction of the total quantity of labour going into a commodity seems, accordingly, to be the essential criterion of increased productivity of labour, no matter under what social conditions production is carried on. Productivity of labour, indeed, would always be measured by this standard in a society in which producers regulate their production according to a preconceived plan."[77]

This economic law, which characterises rational production, is manifested in capitalism as a natural law, that is, as a law of chance (recall the quotation from the first volume of *Capital* quoted earlier), since the value of the commodity in exchange functions as exchange value. Profit, average profit and the market price, as apparently different forms, hide and mystify the same law of value. In this context, it is important to note that production and need meet on the market in the form of supply and demand, and that this meeting comes about in an altogether chance way. It is equally possible that they do not meet; in this event, the law of value is again confirmed as a natural law, but it takes the form of crisis.

People in capitalist society are "accidental individuals", not born into any "natural division of labour"; their destiny is not predetermined from birth. However, given the structure of capitalist society, they are subordinated to a kind of social division of labour that, as we have already said, "allocates" their needs, needs which are no longer determined by their personality but by their position in the social division of labour. At the same time their capacities, "senses" etc. are also "divided" by the social division of labour.

Now let us consider the antinomy of causality and teleology. Engels, following in the footsteps of Hegel, describes the dialectic between human activity and its consequences, by which everyone sets out to realise his own individual ends but the result is something completely different from what the individual originally wanted to achieve. He presents, in a fundamental manner, the contradictory character of commodity-producing society. The fact that he does not recognise it as such but considers it to be "the general dialectical character" of the historical process, spotlights the hegelian foundations of his position. What does the individual capitalist want, what is his goal? He wants the realisation of exchange values, more precisely, to make a profit. And what does the worker want? He wants to survive. These aims are what set the laws of capitalism in motion, "behind the backs of" human beings and the aims which they set for themselves. Even the raising of production is not the aim of an individual. The formula "production for production's sake" which Marx deals with so extensively, is not only a highly scientific formula, it is also a *value judgement* taken from Ricardo. (On the basis of this formula Ricardo justifies capitalism, because it effectively develops the productive forces.) All the same, for the purpose of regulating the mechanism of capitalism it is not the principle "production for production's sake" that counts but the principle "production for the sake of valorising capital". Marx's finest concrete analysis concerning the antinomy of causality and teleology is to be found in the law of the falling average rate of profit. No individual capitalist aims at lowering the average rate of profit. But in order to further his actual aim (to make a profit and to survive under conditions of competition), he must keep increasing his fixed capital and thus constantly submit to the process that causally leads to the continuous lowering of the average rate of profit. In capitalist society, *the individual teleology* can never become *the social teleology*.

Finally, as regards the special antinomy of wealth and poverty (which characterises capitalism in particular) let Marx speak for himself:

"Ricardo, rightly for his time, regards the capitalist mode of production as the most advantageous for production in general, as the most advantageous for the creation of wealth. He wants production for the sake of production and this with good reason. To assert . . . that production as such is not the object, is to forget that production for its own sake means nothing but the development of human productive forces, in other words the development of the richness of human nature as an end in itself. . . . . They reveal a failure to understand the fact that, although at first the development of the capacities of the human species take place at the cost of the majority of the human individuals and even classes, in the end it breaks through this contradiction and coincides with the development of the individual; the higher development of individuality is thus only achieved by a historical process during which individuals are sacrificed."[78]

The discussion here clearly does not turn upon alienation in general, but on capitalist alienation in particular, the alienation of the "pure society" in which commodity relations have become universal and capitalism has "liberated" the productive forces. (See Marx, *Grundrisse*, pp. 157-8, 470 and 528.) For the moment what interests us in particular is the resolution of the antinomy, of the problem of "transition" to the society of the future. What does Marx say? It will be "the development of the capacities of the human species" that breaks through this antagonism. But is this concept synonymous with the "centralisation of the means of production" and the "socialisation of labour" which appear in the passage quoted from the first volume of *Capital*? The answer is, without a doubt, no. The "development of the human species" is a much broader concept than the others; and it is not, of course, a mere consequence of the centralisation of the means of production and the socialisation of labour. Moreover there is no question here (nor in any other passages where this conception of the antinomy is under discussion) of any "natural law" that leads society into the future. The necessity of the "transition" is not in fact "guaranteed" by any *natural* law but by the *radical needs*.

If Marx said that with his first theory of contradiction he "inverted" the dialectic of Hegel, we can justifiably say that with the second he inverted the antinomies of Fichte. The antinomies of freedom and necessity, chance and necessity, causality and teleology, subject and object, are not antinomies in thought but in Being. Nor are they simply antinomies in social Being but rather in commodity-producing society, and in capitalism in particular. According to this interpretation, the dialectic is merely the *expression* of the antinomies in capitalist society. (Following Marx, Lukács interpreted the dialectic in this way in both *History and Class Consciousness* and *The Young Hegel*.)

These, then, are capitalism's "antinomies in Being"; the capitalist "social body" finds expression in them. In *The Poverty of Philosophy* Marx ironically rejects Proudhon's proposal to get rid of the "bad aspects" of capitalism and keep the "good". The structures of the capitalist "formation" are interdependent: it is impossible to reject some and keep others. The specific freedom which stands in a contradictory relation to necessity is not the same as the specific freedom which does not stand in a contradictory relation to necessity. The same applies to necessity in relation to chance, and to teleology in relation to causality. Finally, the specific subject which develops a contradictory relation to its object is not the same as that which "reabsorbs" its object into itself, and which brings about the subject-object identity. (We know in fact that not until "the human species" breaks through capitalist alienation and the antagonistic development of subject and object does the development of the species coincide with that of the individual.)

It is interesting to note the arguments in *The Poverty of Philosophy* from this point of view, where Marx examines every aspect of Proudhon's writing — even down to observing the latter's order of exposition. After the concept of "formation" there follows an important mode of formulation of the radical needs as "the need for universality", which Marx regards as particularly important. The reasoning concludes as follows: "Meanwhile the antagonism between the proletariat and the bourgeoisie is a struggle of class against class, a struggle which carried to its highest expression is a total revolution."[79] That is to say, where there are no "good sides" to preserve in opposition to the "bad sides", where the oppositions are reciprocally arranged and interdependent, total revolution is the only way of transcending this opposing pair.

All this proves what we have been saying up to now. The idea that the transition from capitalism to communism is an objective law of nature is incompatible with Marx's second theory of contradiction. According to this theory, only the revolutionary struggle of the collective subject (the working class), having become such by virtue of its radical needs and revolutionary practice, can guarantee the transition to and creation of the future society.

I have used the word "guarantee" deliberately: it is a "guarantee" in the factual sense of the word. Communism follows from Marx's second theory of contradiction no less necessarily than from his first. In this second theory too, Marx has given Ought an objective existence: as we have already said, not as "natural law" but as the collective Ought. Only the struggle of the collective subject is capable of bringing about the new society: its revolution is radical, "from the root", and total. But the collective Ought arises necessarily, for the "social body" of capitalism itself necessarily generates the radical needs and their bearers. The fact that in Marx's time these radical needs had not yet become actual — at least not on a mass scale — and that Marx therefore had to "invent" them, so to speak, does not disprove the theory. Consider how today we can see with our own eyes the emergence of such "radical needs". It does not detract from Marx's greatness that the bearers of these radical needs today are not, or rather not exclusively, the working class. Marx could only construct radical needs where he saw some possibilities for their development. Another problem is presented by the fact that for us today, the simple "assigning" of Ought to the sphere of objectivity — i.e. the idea of the necessity of revolutionary action — cannot be accepted, for we would at least have to add Engels's qualification: "on pain of death".

I have said that in the society of associated producers which Marx foresaw the above-mentioned antinomies cease to exist, and that the way to overcome them is total revolution. How, in Marx's view, is communist society shaped from the point of view of overcoming these particular antinomies? I shall deal with it only in a few words here, because the analysis of the system of needs in the society of associated producers will come later. When the opposition between subject and object ceases, as we have already seen, the wealth of the species and the wealth of the individual "coincide" (*Economic and Philosophic Manuscripts of*

1844), i.e. the wealth of the species is represented by every separate individual. The realm of production (the organic interchange between society and nature) remains the realm of necessity, but necessity is subordinated to freedom. Social relations between human beings then become free relations; mankind, socialised in freedom, dominates the realm of necessity and regulates it, controls it. The law of value does not assert itself on the market: hence the aspect of chance is eliminated from the economy. Human beings no longer have a chance relationship with society. As socialised individuals, they represent the human species for itself. Teleology has dominance over causality. The "associated intelligence" of the associated producers embodies social teleology. No quasi-natural force makes itself felt "behind the backs of people": from the dispositions of the collective teleology, what people *really want* "emerges". The subordination to which we refer will be possible only because the freedom, necessity, teleology and social wealth of the future society are not the same freedom, necessity, teleology and wealth as in capitalist society. The future society, in every aspect of its structure, is fundamentally different from capitalist society, and hence it can only come about in total revolution. However, it is obviously the capitalist development of the productive forces that generates the possibility of this revolution.

This latter feature is common to both of Marx's conceptions of contradiction. One observation seems necessary here. In my own view it has been sufficiently proved that in Marx there are two kinds of theory of contradiction which are mutually exclusive in principle; but this does not mean that there are no passages in Marx's work where the two conceptions appear together, where in dealing with one theory of contradiction considerations deriving from the other are also used. There are actually several such examples. I have already drawn attention to it: we saw that in "the negation of the negation" there is an echo of the "radical needs" motif, though in this particular context the motif was not essential.

The fact that Marx held two differing theories of contradiction is not a defect in his thought: on the contrary, it is a striking proof of his genius. Like every other thinker of importance, he too refused to sacrifice the *search* for truth in various directions and along various paths on the altar of coherence. He pinpointed various possibilities of finding a solution and considered every one of them with the consistency that is characteristic of genius. To refurbish Marx into a thinker who worked out a coherent system means to deprive him of precisely the main source of his greatness: his feverish and many-sided search for truth. It is characteristic of a great thinker that he not only creates important impulses, but that these impulses point in many directions. The immortality, the living content of Marx's thought which transcends historical epochs, is based precisely upon this brilliant lack of coherence. For this reason it is always possible to rediscover him; for this reason many different movements, which however are all of world historical importance, can consider Marx as their precursor, as "their own". His work is a clear, inexhausible fountain.

The conception of radical needs appears for the first time in a detailed form in the Introduction to (the proposed revision of) A Critique of Hegel's "Philosophy of Law". If we look at this conception in the course of its birth, we can "catch it red-handed": we can see how far Marx gives Ought an objective existence, when he says that pure theoretical critique is realised in activity, in tasks "for whose solution there is one means only: practice". The reference goes further:

"The weapon of criticism obviously cannot replace the criticism of weapons. Material force must be overthrown by material force. But theory also becomes a material force once it has gripped the masses. Theory is capable of gripping the masses when it demonstrates ad hominem, and it demonstrates ad hominem when it becomes radical. To be radical is to grasp things by the root, but for man the root is man himself."[80]

Marx measures the radicalism of theory in terms of the way it attributes value (i.e. its value-premise): theory is radical to the extent that man (human wealth) represents the highest value. (I do not consider this value-premise to be characteristic only of the younger Marx, as I have already pointed out several times. We need only look at the third volume of Theories of Surplus Value, where Marx quotes the expression used by Galiani, "true wealth . . . is man", and praises with enthusiasm rare for him the sublime "idealism" of the proletarian ideology expressed there.)

The problem is, however, as follows: how can radical theory become practice? How can it grip the masses? How can the values of radical criticism become the values of the masses, that is, how can Ought become the collective Ought? The reply is: "Theory is actualised in a people only in so far as it actualises *their needs.* . . . *A deep-going revolution can only be a revolution in basic needs.*" The "bearers" of radical needs are therefore those who can actualise radical deep-going theory. Marx then looks for the bearers of these radical needs and in the end he finds them in the working class. He bases his conclusion on the fact that it is "a class with radical chains, a class in civil society that is not of civil society . . . a sphere of society having a universal character because of its universal suffering and claiming no particular right because no particular wrong but unqualified wrong is perpetrated on it; a sphere that can invoke no traditional title but only a human title."[81] The working class therefore embodies radical needs, because it has no *particular* goals of its own, nor can it have any, since its goals, by the very fact of being the working class's goals, can only be general. Later on Marx speaks again of this idea — for example, in *The Communist Manifesto* — saying that the working class cannot free itself without freeing humanity as a whole. (*The Communist Manifesto* is, on the other hand, also the work in which the concept of class interest is introduced. Since it was written jointly by Marx and Engels, I have not taken it into consideration in my analysis of interest.)

If indeed it is right to say — and in my opinion it is — that the working class can free itself only by freeing humanity too, it does not follow from this however that in terms of historical reality the working class actually wishes to free itself and that its needs are in fact radical needs. Nor does it even follow that it has no particular goals (particular needs) which it can realise or satisfy within capitalist society. As we have seen, Marx himself speaks later on of these particular interests in relation to the struggle for wages: he contrasts the particular struggle for wage increases with the "general" struggle to abolish the wages system and to satisfy radical needs. Remember also that, in Marx's view, what characterises the working class is both its reduction to paltry particular needs and interests, and at the same time the rise of radical needs.

In his subsequent writings, Marx no longer seeks the origin of "radical needs" either in "radical chains" or in the absence of particular goals. But the essence of his viewpoint remains unchanged. It is based on the fact that capitalist society itself gives rise to radical needs, thus producing its own gravediggers, and that these needs are an organic constituent part of the "social body" of capitalism, thus being unsatisfiable within that society; for precisely this reason, they are the motives of the practice which transcends the given society.

In *The German Ideology* radical needs are founded on what for the proletariat has *accidentally* become labour, "over which the individual proletarians have no control and over which no *social* organisation can give any control; and the contradiction between the personality of the individual proletarian and the condition of life that is imposed upon him, labour, is clear to the proletarian himself."[82] (It emerges clearly from this quotation that the idea of radical needs proceeds from Marx's *second* theory of contradiction.)

According to Marx, therefore, the worker becomes *conscious* of the contradiction between the need to develop his personality and the "accidental" character of his subordination to the division of labour. For this very reason,

"Proletarians, *in order to make themselves felt as persons*, must abolish their own conditions of existence as they have been up to the present, which at the same time are the conditions of existence for all society up to the present time, namely labour [read "wage labour" — A.H.]. So they find themselves also in direct antagonism with the form in which individuals in society have up to now found their collective expression, the state, and they *must overturn the state* to express *their own* personality."[83]

It is necessary to observe that in this passage the word "must" appears twice and on both occasions is stressed. This necessity is not, however, that of "objectively natural economic laws" but of subjective action, of collective activity, of practice.

The idea that radical needs are in some sense constituted from labour runs like a thread through Marx's work: either because surplus labour (performed for its own sake) becomes need; or because of the increase in free time, which gives rise to radical needs (and to the need for still more free time); or because of the need for universality which, having arisen in the form of mass production, cannot be satisfied within capitalism.

The need for free time is, in Marx's view, an elemental one, because it always thrusts beyond the limits of alienation. In the first volume of *Capital* and elsewhere, the struggle for more free time (for a decrease in labour time) constantly appears within the focus of the proletarian class struggle:

"There is here, therefore, an antinomy, law against law, both equally bearing the seal of the law of exchange. It is *force* that decides between equal laws. Hence the fact that in the history of capitalist production, the determination of the length of the working day presents itself as the result of a struggle for its limitation: a struggle between the collective capitalist, i.e. the capitalist class, and the collective labourer, i.e. the working class."[84]

While the wage struggle, according to Marx, is conducted for the particular interests of the proletariat, the struggle for free time transcends particular interests and contains in principle "that which conforms to the needs of the species". He proudly draws attention to the fact that when workers were asked in the course of a sociological survey whether they wanted more wages or more free time, the great majority opted for the latter. Of course, he does not deny that the struggle for free time can also remain within the framework of capitalism. But it is precisely the laws regulating commodity exchange that give rise to the "equal laws" between which force decides. At the same time, he is convinced that from a certain point onwards capitalism is incapable of shortening labour time any further: the need for free time then becomes in principle a radical need, which can only be satisfied with the transcendence of capitalism. When related to the need for free time, the character of "radical needs" is brought out in a particularly striking manner: it is produced by capitalism itself, by its contradictory character, and thus belongs to the very functioning of capitalism. (The reduction of labour time compels capitalists to increase their productivity constantly, and to give priority to relative rather than absolute surplus value; this basically represents a specific peculiarity of the capitalist production of surplus value.) At the same time, need itself mobilises the working class into transcending capitalism.

The same applies to the need for universality. In *The German*

91

Ideology, this idea is still openly formulated with its characteristic of "Ought". The need for universality *must* come about, because only people who have become possessed of the need (and the capacity) for universality are capable of a total revolution:

"Private property can be abolished only on condition of an all-round development of individuals, because the existing character of intercourse and productive forces is an all-round one, and *only individuals that are developing in an all-round fashion* can appropriate them, i.e. can turn them into free manifestations of their lives."[85]

But in *The Poverty of Philosophy* Marx no longer refers to Ought. The need for universality has already come about, in capitalism; the "radical need" to transcend capitalism already "exists":

"What characterises the division of labour in the automatic workshop is that labour has there completely lost its specialised character. But the moment every special development stops, the need for universality, the tendency towards an integral development of the individual begins to be felt."[86]

Marx expresses the same idea in the first volume of *Capital*. The "machine" that dominates in capitalist society makes the development of a universality of capacities indispensable. But while in capitalist society this tendency asserts itself as a natural law, the capitalist division of labour nevertheless "serves as a barrier" to the development of universality. In order to realise this universality (no longer as a natural law asserting itself behind the backs of human beings), the working class must conquer political power and overcome the division of labour.

"But if, on the one hand, the variation of work at present imposes itself after the manner of an overpowering natural law, and *with the blindly destructive action of a natural law* that meets with resistance at all points, modern industry, on the other hand, through its catastrophies imposes the necessity of recognising, as a fundamental law of production, the variation of work, and consequently fitness of the labourer for varied work, and consequently the greatest possible development of his varied aptitudes. It becomes a question of life and death for society to adapt the mode of production to the normal functioning of this law. Modern industry, indeed, compels society, under penalty of death, to replace the detail-worker of today, crippled by life-long repetition of one and the same trivial operation, and thus reduced to the mere fragment of a man, by the fully developed individual, fit for a variety of labours, ready to face any change of production, and to whom the different social functions he performs are but so many modes of giving free scope to his own natural and acquiring powers. . . . There can be no doubt that when the working class comes into power, as *inevitably* it must, technical instruction, both theoretical and practical, will take its proper place in the working-class schools. There is also no doubt that such revolutionary ferments, the final result of which is the abolition of the old division of labour, are *diametrically opposed* to the capitalist form of production, and to the economic status of the labourer corresponding to that form."[87]

Undoubtedly Marx here is raising only one aspect of the problem of radical needs, giving a meaning to the concept that is more limited than in the previously quoted passages. But the mature Marx does not consider radical needs only from this point of view. Moreover he deals with the same problem, in relation to the dissolution of the family, barely two pages after the passage quoted, where he says that capitalism dissolves the Germano-Christian family form as a "combination of working personnel, composed of individuals of both sexes and all ages, which *must* (under the relevant conditions) become a source of *humane* development, although in its spontaneously developed, brutal, capitalistic form, where *the labourer exists for the process of production and not the process of production for the labourer,* it is a pestiferous source of corruption and slavery."[88]

It would be a mistake, however, to think that the mature Marx relates the structure of radical needs exclusively to modern industrial production. In the *Grundrisse* the idea of radical needs has a more universal character than in any of the earlier works. He maintains there that capitalist alienation itself gives rise to radical needs, because of the very consciousness of alienation:

"The material which it works on [Marx is referring here to subjective "labour capacity", not to the workers — A.H.] is alien material; the instrument is likewise an alien instrument; its labour appears as a mere accessory to their substance and hence objectifies itself in things not belonging to it. Indeed, living labour itself appears as alien vis-à-vis living labour capa-

93

city, whose labour it is, whose own life's expression it is. . . . Labour capacity relates to its labour as to an alien, and if capital were willing to pay it without making it labour it would enter the bargain with pleasure. Thus labour capacity's own labour is as alien to it — and it really is, as regards its direction etc. — as are material and instrument. Which is why the product then appears to it as a combination of alien material, alien instrument and alien labour — as alien property, . . . the recognition of the products as its own and the judgement that its separation from the conditions of its realisation is improper — forcibly imposed — is a consciousness *which exceeds its bounds*, itself the product of the mode of production resting on capital and as much the knell to its doom as, with the slave's consciousness that he cannot be the property of another, with his consciousness of himself as a person, the existence of slavery becomes a merely artificial, vegetative existence, and ceases to be able to prevail as the basis of production."[89]

Here every aspect of Marx's conception appears clearly and unequivocally.

(1) Capitalism is an antinomous society: its essence is alienation. The wealth of the species and the poverty of the individual are reciprocally based and reproduce each other. The antinomy is that of *commodity* production *becoming universal*. (At the beginning of the paragraph quoted, Marx says: "Value having become capital, and living labour confronting it as mere use value, so that living labour appears as a mere means to realise objectified, dead labour . . . , and having produced, as the end product, alien wealth on one side and, on the other, the penury which is living labour capacity's sole possession."[90])

(2) Capitalist society as a totality, as a "social body", produces not only alienation but the consciousness of alienation, in other words, radical needs.

(3) This consciousness (radical needs) is necessarily generated by capitalism.

(4) This consciousness (the complex of radical needs) already transcends capitalism by its existence, and its development makes it impossible for capitalism to remain the basis of production. The need to resolve the antinomy and the activity directed towards this end are therefore constituted in the collective

94

Ought, in the consciousness that "exceeds its bounds" [*enorme Bewusstsein*].

This concept of "consciousness exceeding its bounds" is beyond question the same as the "imputed consciousness" [*zugerechnete Bewusstsein*] which is a central category in Lukács's *History and Class Consciousness* (and nothing shows Lukács's insight into Marx's ideas better than the fact that he did not know the *Grundrisse* when he wrote his own book). Although Marx does not say so, it is obvious that this "consciousness exceeding its bounds" is not identical with the "empirical consciousness" of the working class. It is not consciousness of misery and still less of poverty in the narrow sense: the needs which flow from it (or which constitute its base) are not directed towards "greater possession" and still less towards higher wages or a "better standard of living". It is the simple consciousness of alienation, the recognition that the social relations are alienated: from this there follows (or this constitutes the base for) the need to overcome alienation, to overturn the alienated social and productive relations in a revolutionary way, and to create general social and productive relations which are not alienated.

As yet, history has not answered the question as to whether capitalist society *in fact* produces this "consciousness exceeding its bounds", which in Marx's day did not exist, and whose existence Marx therefore had to *project*.

V

The "System of Needs" and the "Society of Associated Producers"

Marx's analysis of the society of associated producers is philosophically founded upon the concept of the *system of needs*. From the philosophical point of view, individual concrete needs cannot be analysed in isolation, since neither isolated needs nor isolated types of need exist. Every society has its own characteristic system of needs, which is therefore in no way valid for judging the system of needs of another society. "Is the entire *system of needs* founded on estimation or on the whole organisation of production? Most often, needs arise directly from *production* or from a *state of affairs* based on production."[91] Here I shall briefly summarise Marx's description of the dominant system of needs in capitalism (I have already spoken of it in the second chapter). The structure of needs is reduced to the need for possession, which subordinates the entire system to itself. All this is manifested in the members of the ruling class as the need quantitatively to increase needs of a single quality and the objects with which to satisfy these needs, whilst in the working class it is manifested as the reduction to simple needs of existence, that is to "natural needs" and to their satisfaction. Qualitative needs are quantified; needs as ends are turned into needs as means and vice versa. Since needs of heterogeneous qualities cannot develop, men's pleasures remain "crude" and "brutal", and some of their needs become "fixed". Relations of interest dominate relationships between human beings.

Production, the relations of production, social relations and systems of needs are, as we know, different aspects of a single formation, in which each is the precondition of the other. The structure of needs is an organic structure inherent in the total social formation. The structure of needs in capitalist society belongs therefore exclusively to *capitalist* society. It cannot be used to judge any other society in general and least of all that of "the associated producers", since the latter is the opposite not only of capitalist society but of every civilised society that has existed to date; it is the first non-alienated society, "the realm of freedom".

But if a system of needs is specific to a given social formation, how can the subjective forces arise which are to overturn this given society? Every (civilised) society is a *class* society founded upon the division of labour, in which there is also a "division" in the system of needs. The exploited classes generally ask for no more than a better satisfaction of the needs assigned to them. However, these same exploited masses become conscious (in various different historical conditions) of the existing opposition between their needs and those of the dominant classes. In this case they seek to get rid of everything that stands in the way of the satisfaction of their needs and to make their own system of needs general, as well as to make certain aspects of the ruling class's system of needs realisable for themselves. This leads either to the overturning of the social order or to the general ruin of the productive forces. In the first event a new ruling class organises itself (and the way in which the bourgeois state arose is the classic example of this); in the second case society is unable to function (in the passage cited from the *Grundrisse*, Marx interprets the fall of the Roman Empire in this latter sense).

Needs that transcend the present in this sense, however, are not radical needs. This is because need does not transcend the system of needs as a whole but only the "division" of it. The need of the slave to be a free man is not a new need, because the society that enslaves him is a society of free men. The bourgeoisie's need to take political power is likewise not a new need; it is simply a demand for the satisfaction of a need which is already available to others, and for the elimination of the obstacles to this satisfaction. The radical needs of the working class created by capitalism are, however, different by definition. Their nature is such that they cannot previously have been satisfied in the given society, either by the bourgeoisie or by the proletariat. (The Being of the bourgeoisie is just as alienated as that of the proletariat.)

Therefore it is exclusively the radical needs which lead to the complete restructuring of the system of needs; on this, Marx has no doubts whatever. The system of needs under capitalism

97

belongs to capitalism. But it is precisely this "pure" society which, by developing the productive forces sufficiently to overcome the division of labour, can and does create needs that belong to its Being but do not belong to its system of needs. Thus only the radical needs enable man, in the interests of satisfying them, to bring about a social formation which is *radically*, "from the root", different from the previous one, a society in which the radically new system of needs will be different from all earlier ones.

It is therefore absurd to try to use the current, existing structure of needs as a basis for judging the system of needs which is Marx's precondition for the society of associated producers. Without the concept of restructuring the system of needs, the assertion that labour and surplus value will become a vital need is simply incomprehensible. For Marx, the complete restructuring of the system of needs in communism is the *sine qua non* for any assertion about the future society. One can already read, in the *Economic and Philosophic Manuscripts of 1844*, that even the "senses" of "socialised" human beings will be different from what they are now. In the *Grundrisse*, Marx writes about the development of the wealth of human life in free time: "Free time — which is both idle time and time for higher activity — has *naturally* transformed its possessor into a different subject."[92] (The stimulus for Marx to discuss this problem more deeply arises from the question of "natural" and "luxury" needs, that is, the question of overcoming the opposition between them. "These questions about *the system of needs* . . . — at what point is this to be dealt with?"[93]) Marx regards the radical restructuring of needs, capacities and senses as "natural". But since the society of associated producers also represents a totality, a "social formation" just as every other society does, the foundations of its operative mechanism and of the radically new structure of needs are interdependent. The new system of needs therefore becomes comprehensible only in relation to the functioning of the new social body, just as the functioning of the new social "formation" as a whole is comprehensible only in relation to the new system of needs.

The "society of associated producers" is thus the society in which radical needs come to be satisfied, and around which a new structure of needs is built. It is therefore also a society in which radical philosophy and radical theory are realised and surmounted. (This does not, of course, mean the unqualified surmounting of philosophy as such, but of the radical philosophy which must grip the masses in order to become a material force. This will become clearer later on.)

The system of needs in communism must be dealt with from two distinct aspects: from that of material and non-material needs, and from that of the relation between these two types within a single structure of needs. By "material needs" I mean needs whose objects and means of satisfaction (used in consumption and in productive consumption) must be produced and continually reproduced. Needs of a non-material character are, in contrast, those whose objects of satisfaction are not "produced" in the organic interchange with nature or are not produced at all. (I know that this is not a "pure" distinction. To satisfy the need for art, production is to some extent necessary: houses must be built, books must be printed. But the need for art as such is not satisfied either by the house or by the book but by the *work of art*, which as an objectivation does not belong to the sphere of production.) The distinction between these two aspects is not arbitrary. It is based on an essential distinction which Marx applied. In his view, the sphere of production is the field which will always remain "the realm of necessity"; above it is the "realm of freedom", which subordinates production to its own ends. Needs that can be satisfied only through institutions (this also applies to social and community satisfaction of needs) are partly of a material nature, since they absorb material means, and partly not, since they are satisfied by human activity (Marx cites schools and hospitals as examples). The need for public institutions is partly of a material nature (for example, the construction of dwellings) and partly not (rendering services of a non-material nature). For Marx, at least in the "second phase" of communism, this is natural, since the opposition between productive and unproductive labour, which is constituted by capitalism, ceases to exist, since there is no longer either exchange or exchange value, labour power is not a commodity, etc. The category of "socially necessary labour time" will be interpretable only in relation to the process of material production. (The concept of "socially necessary labour time" is not applicable to any "free" activity, whether medicine, teaching, planning, or scientific and artistic activity.) Certainly, all this does not hold true for "the first phase of communism", in so far as the division there is regulated on the basis of labour supplied, for which "the socially necessary labour time" must obviously be measured in every activity involving labour. On this point Marx does not give any detailed analysis, limiting himself simply to the observation that in this phase the system of equal rights for unequal individuals prevails, i.e. the legal system of bourgeois society. We cannot imagine this mechanism without commodity and money relations. In the well known tenth paragraph of *The Communist Manifesto*, which describes the measures necessary for laying the basis for the first phase of communism, there is no hint of the overcoming of commodity production. Marx and Engels speak only of "measures . . . which appear economically insufficient and untenable, but which, in the course of the movement, outstrip themselves, necessitate further inroads upon the old social order and are unavoidable as a means of entirely revolutionising the mode of production."[94] In the eyes of Marx and Engels this transition appears as inevitable, and they do not take the actual problems into consideration. Likewise, it is unclear whether the realisation of the first phase of communism also brings with it the overcoming of commodity production, or whether this will be characteristic of the second phase. Marx and Engels rarely deal with the "how"? of the transition; they limit themselves to the comparison of "ideal types". Since we are analysing Marx's theory of need, we too can work only with these "ideal types". We are therefore forced to exclude a problem which is crucial for us today, namely the problem of transition (which of course can last for centuries), and to refrain from analysing his model of transition, or rather his possible models. It is necessary also to make another limitation: given that we are analysing Marx's theory of needs, we shall consider the model of "associated producers" only from this latter point of view and leave the other aspects aside, important as they may be.

To be able to analyse the relationship of needs to material production and its products, we must also find out exactly what role is played by material production in Marx's idea of the "society of associated producers". We need to examine the following aspects:

(a) Is production developed?

(b) To what extent does the development of production represent the growth of "social wealth"?

(c) Is there a division of labour?

(d) Do necessary and surplus labour exist or not?

(e) What are the proportions between the production of direct consumer goods and means of production on the one hand, and the production of those goods which are essential for the "social satisfaction of needs" on the other?

To the first question, Marx's reply is an unequivocal yes. The society of the future is also a society of material wealth, which continues to grow. This idea is encountered in virtually all of Marx's works. I shall cite just one example as proof. In the third volume of *Theories of Surplus Value,* he describes the two alternatives for increasing "disposable time". One alternative would be to produce greater wealth in half the current average labour time. The other would be to reduce the labour time by half in such a way as to direct the remaining half towards the satisfaction of "necessary needs" as they are at present. Marx considers it a theoretical mistake, a lack of clarity, to confuse these two alternatives. He explicitly declares himself to be in favour of the first of them.

The base for the future development of production will be the extraordinary growth in the proportion of fixed capital, which is quite possible because the increase in production will be independent of the valorisation of capital. The increase in the proportion of fixed capital to levels that are impossible under capitalism is the guarantee that material production will require ever less living labour. This is the only way to reduce labour time uninterruptedly whilst maintaining a constant increase in production. This does not of course mean that dead labour will dominate living labour (because the capital relation no longer exists); on the contrary, living labour will prevail over dead.

The idea of unlimited progress in material production is a clear characteristic of Marx's thought; his ideas on the *rate* of increase of production are, however, contradictory on more than one occasion. On the one hand, he assumes that capitalism arrives at a point where the development of the forces of production (and

101

in particular the increase in fixed capital) ceases, and that therefore the rate of material production in the society of associated producers would have to be more rapid, at least in comparison with the situation in latter-day capitalism. On the other hand, the increased rate of material production (which we shall have more to say about later) is determined by the needs of the associated producers. However, in parallel with the growing wealth, these needs will be less and less directed towards material consumer goods. This already suggests a new structure of needs which is of decisive importance. In the new structure of needs, Marx uses a sort of "saturation model": material consumer goods (those which serve immediate consumption) would play an increasingly limited role in the structure of needs of individuals, or at any rate their proportion would be less. They would be limited by other needs, not by production itself, since production does not overtake needs but is directed towards them. On the basis of the model indicated, it is in fact inconceivable that any new material needs could arise from production itself, i.e. that new types of need could be "produced". All this should indicate a fall-off in the rate of increase of production, at least after a certain level of wealth is attained.

Marx believed that he could already see this "structural change", in the "radical needs" of the proletariat of his day. This can also be seen from his comments on the theses of the proletarian ideologist, Galiani. The latter's basic thesis was, as we know, that "true wealth . . . is man". Marx supported this view, and added: "The whole objective world, the 'world of goods', vanishes here as a mere aspect . . . of socially producing men."[95]

And so we come to the second problem. To what extent does the development of production represent the growth of "social wealth"? We can extract two quite distinct problems from this question (though they usually appear together):

1) To what extent can *labour* be considered the source of material wealth?
2) To what extent can *production* (including the material wealth which is realised in production) be considered the sole source of wealth in general?

It should be pointed out that Marx regards the two questions as completely separable in principle, mainly because the source of use values (wealth in use values being actual material wealth) is labour *and* nature, not labour alone. (A radical analysis of this problem can be found in the *Critique of the Gotha Programme* and elsewhere.)

(1) Marx gives different answers to the first question, which we shall consider in due course.

It is bourgeois society which considers labour to be the only source of material wealth, a society dominated by the contradiction between use value and exchange value which is embodied in commodity production. (In *Theories of Surplus Value*, Marx accuses some of Ricardo's critics of remaining within the system of categories of bourgeois society, in that they still consider labour the sole source of wealth even when they draw conclusions from this which are opposed to those of Ricardo.) Still more important, however, is the fact that according to Marx's conception of labour, the labour performed in production in the society of associated producers decreases to a minimum and even ceases to exist. It becomes, therefore, absurd to see labour as the source of (material) wealth, or to apply the criterion of labour time to (material) wealth. In developing this position, Marx adopts — albeit with some reservations — the reasoning of the author of the booklet "Source and Remedy": this does not alter the fact that it is also his own position. I would, however, stress that this is only one of Marx's conceptions, which demonstrates all the more that in his eyes the statements "labour is the source of material wealth" and "production is the source of material wealth" are different and clearly distinguishable from each other.

In this connection I would like also to quote from the *Grundrisse*:

"Labour no longer appears so much to be included within the production process; rather, the human being comes to relate more as watchman and regulator to the production process itself. . . . No longer does the worker insert a modified natural thing as middle link between the object and himself; rather, he inserts the process of Nature, transformed into an industrial process, as a means between himself and inorganic Nature, mastering it. He steps to the side of the production process instead of being its chief actor. In this transformation, it is neither the direct human labour he himself performs, nor the time during which he works, but rather the appropriation of his own general productive power, his understanding of nature and his mastery over it by virtue of his presence as a social body — it is, in a word, the development of the social individual which appears as the great foundation-stone of production and of wealth. . . . As soon as labour in the direct form has ceased to be the great well-spring of wealth, labour time ceases and must cease to be its measure, and hence exchange value must cease to be the measure of use value."[96]

Let us disregard for the moment the fact that Marx identifies value with exchange value here, concepts which he rigorously separates in *Capital*, where he is using a different conception of labour (in which the measure of labour time necessarily plays a part). We shall analyse this passage only for our own purposes. The "society of associated producers" appears in this quotation as a society in which labour is carried out by machines, in which "fixed capital" therefore completely predominates and in which — at least in the process of material production — labour power is employed only "as watchman and regulator". To use a modern expression, Marx presupposes complete automation. In this way a specific type of labour acquires an extraordinary importance, namely, scientific labour, or (as Marx calls it) "labour in general". Scientific labour is not, however, immediately productive labour, but the activity of the general intellect: planning, projection and so forth. This cannot however be measured in labour time, since the concept of "socially necessary labour time" is not applicable. In short, material wealth is still supplied by production, but no longer by productive labour in the conventional sense of the term. This determines the hegemony of intellectual labour over so-called "physical" labour.

(2) The other question is whether production is the source of wealth in society. Marx replies everywhere and unequivocally, no. The material wealth which comes about through production is not and cannot be anything but a *condition* of the general wealth of society. The true wealth of society is realised through the free self-activity of social individuals and through their qualitatively many-sided system of needs. The true wealth of man and society consists not in labour time but in *free time*. For this very reason the wealth of the society of associated producers cannot be measured by labour but only by free time. I shall here refer

104

not to the well known passages in the *Grundrisse*, but to the third volume of *Theories of Surplus Value*:

"Labour time, even if exchange value is eliminated, always remains the creative substance of wealth and the meaasure of the cost of its production. But free time, disposable time, is wealth itself, partly for the enjoyment of the product, partly for the free activity which — unlike labour — is not dominated by the pressure of an extraneous purpose which must be fulfilled, and the fulfilment of which is regarded as a natural necessity or a social duty, according to one's inclination."[97]

(This passage presupposes the distinction between exchange value and value.)

Both (1) and (2), different as they are, are solutions which presuppose a change in the structure of needs, so that individuals feel the need for more free time (and for "free activity" in it) rather than for a further increase in the production of goods and material wealth. (There is in fact no level of production which is so high that one cannot — at the expense of free time — produce still more.) In both conceptions you find the conviction at its most profound: that needs in the "society of associated producers" have limits set to them by other, qualitatively different needs. (We shall come back again to the part played by "general labour" in these models, as well as to the problem of the need for free time.)

The relationship between material production and the structure of needs in the society of associated producers is purely a function of the existence or non-existence of the division of labour and, if it does exist, of its nature.

(1) Without doubt the social division of labour will cease, and with it the division of society into exploiters and exploited; in a word, the class structure. The "dividing out" which takes place in the system of needs according to the position occupied in the social division of labour will also cease. The individual will no longer be subordinated to the social division of labour. Thus if a division of labour continues to exist in another sense of the term, the individual will however be able to choose freely the position he wishes to occupy and will *always* be able to renew his choice. In principle this is also the case in capitalism, but in fact it has never been so: the social division of labour subordinates

man to itself and in practice people cannot "choose" any work except that which they *have to* perform. The continual "change" of work under capitalism is not the consequence of the worker's free choice or of his "needs for development" but is subordinated to the need to valorise capital. If we suppose that in the society of associated producers there needs to be at least some kind of division of labour, then the entry into this division and the changes of work will depend only on the worker's "needs for development".

(2) The division between manual and intellectual *labour* will clearly be overcome. Marx had two different conceptions of how this might come about.

We have already mentioned one of these: production and labour are separated; man "sets himself alongside the process of production"; every activity of the worker (including those which are socially necessary) becomes labour of an intellectual type.

The other conception that Marx introduces is essentially different: on the basis of it (as we shall see later on) every type of productive labour comes to be reduced to simple labour. However, here too labour time must be reduced so that human life can be engaged for the most part in intellectual activity. But intellectual activity is also, at least in part, labour (it involves fatigue and uses the brain, nerves, strength, muscles — particularly the first two). In both types of labour the opposition between *work* and *labour* disappears; this opposition reaches its culminating point in capitalism and is characteristic of class society.[*] In the labour that is performed in "socially necessary labour time", work guides labour (recall the last phrase in the passage quoted from *Theories of Surplus Value*: labour will always be subjected to external ends, but — in contradistinction to what happens in capitalism — men will perform it as "social duty"). But this distinction will finally disappear in the labour of "free activity": work becomes "pure" labour.

If, however, "labour" in this latter sense and physical labour — the two things are distinct, in both of Marx's conceptions — are given (and indeed, this "labour" is a constant in both con-

---

[*]For the distinction (and the opposition) between work and labour see the chapter on labour in my book *A Mindennapi Elet* ("Everyday Life").

106

ceptions), then they will be performed by all, and so every person will have time (equal amounts of time) for "free activity". According to the first conception, the very nature of "labour" will do away with the distinction between manual and intellectual labour; according to the other, this will not be the case. As far as individuals are concerned, however, Marx's thinking is coherent and unambiguous: every human being will take part in the process of interaction between nature and society. In other words, as long as manual labour exists it will be performed; if it does not exist, the functioning of fixed capital will be "regulated". But every human being will perform highly developed, purely intellectual labour. This is the essence of the young Marx's extraordinarily perceptive remark that under communism the human being will be fisherman, hunter, shepherd and critical critic, and that there will be no such people as "painters" but simply those who, among other things, paint. So according to Marx's view of the future, there will in effect be no specialised workers involved in "purely intellectual" or "purely manual" activities. This does not mean, however, that there will be no specialised intellectual activity in productive labour or in the control of production: it simply means that the specialised activity performed in production does not determine the direction of a person's intellectual activity during their free time, and that it does not determine their chosen form of self-realisation. And it does not negate the principle that anyone may give priority to any particular form of activity during their free time: it simply means that they must participate in "labour", in the performance of socially necessary labour and in the regulation and control of production. Real theoretical problems arise, however, for Marx does not discuss the question of whether one has to produce in order to perform free-time activities. According to the conception of "the measurement of needs" (which we shall deal with later), material consumption (direct and productive consumption) requires material production. But nothing is said about "free activity". This explains why it is so easy for Marx to measure material needs and to calculate their "average".

(3) We have examined the way in which various forms of the division of labour are overcome: but this does not explain how *every* division of labour is overcome. Marx quite clearly says that there will be a technical division of labour (though only one) in

the society of associated producers. One reads in *Capital*, for example, that the whole of social production will function as a single factory, with the division of social labour corresponding to the technical division of labour in a factory. In the third volume of *Theories of Surplus Value*, he specifically raises the question of whether the concentration of capital and the continued growth of fixed capital, which makes the technical division of labour necessary, do not also entail a necessity for capitalist relations of production and a social division of labour. And in this context, Marx attacks those theoreticians who tie the specialisation which arises from centralisation to capitalist relations of production, "as if the division of labour were not *likewise* possible if *its conditions belonged to the associated workers,* and were regarded by the latter as their own products and the material elements of their own activity, which they are by their very nature."[98] What the bourgeois economists want to achieve with this identification is "a technological justification for the specific social form, i.e. the capitalist form, in which the relationship of labour to the conditions of labour is turned upside down, so that it is not the worker who makes use of the conditions of labour, but the conditions of labour which make use of the worker."[99]

What does the presence of the technical division of labour mean for human labour? How can it guarantee the universality of mankind? Is individual specialisation possible within it? Marx's only consistent reply to these questions is in *Capital*. Other solutions appear only in the form of aphorisms: when he says that man will be at one and the same time fisherman, hunter, shepherd and critical critic, Marx has in mind a Goethean universality, even if he does not mean that man can be a dilettante in everything; he means rather that man can excel in many kinds of activity which are basically different as regards their quality. In *Capital*, on the other hand, he means that all labour will be reduced to a simple labour which is easy to learn and to perform. The pespective of universality in this case does not mean — at least where the labour process is concerned — that people may excel in various fields, but that they can always "change" their work, without having specific qualifications. In the *Grundrisse* the activity of man who appears "alongside the process of production" is complex and calls for qualification. However, Marx does not go deeply into this conception; the important thing for us is that he does not apply it to the analysis of the relationship between productive labour and material needs. Clearly, therefore, the structure of needs sketched in the model in the *Grundrisse* cannot be the same as that in *Capital*. Since I am analysing only the explicit positions that Marx takes, it is necessary to keep to the arguments concerning this problem in *Capital*.

The validity of the categories of "necessary labour" and "surplus labour" in the society of associated producers, and the interpretation of the category of "socially necessary labour", are crucially dependent on the question of whether Marx identifies value and exchange value or whether he differentiates between them. Up to and including *A Contribution to the Critique of Political Economy* he tends to regard them as synonymous. But later he works with two concepts of value. The first keeps the earlier meaning: value is realised exclusively in the exchange relation (see *Capital*, Vol. 1, page 60). According to the other interpretation, value is a general social category (at least in a rational economy); the law of value is a *general* economic law which, as we have seen, can find an adequate expression only in "the society of associated producers". (Remember the arguments in the first volume of *Capital*, with which Marx demonstrates that "the mystical form" of the commodity cannot have originated either from use value or from value [see *Capital*, Vol. 1, page 72-3].) In this connection a passage from the *Critique of the Gotha Programme* of 1875 is also relevant. In it, Marx speaks of how and when distribution according to needs can be realised. He explicitly says that value exists only in the first phase of communism, where goods cannot yet be distributed according to needs. Where there is value, distribution takes place according to labour. The first phase of communism is thus still marked by the equality of exchange: equal labour is exchanged for equal labour. Labour must still be measured on the basis of labour time (quantitatively and qualitatively equal labour times are exchanged). However, "within the co-operative society based on common ownership of the means of production, the producers do not exchange their products, any more than the labour employed on the products appears as the *value* of them."[100] One might of course interpret this as meaning that value ceases to exist only in the first meaning of the concept:

but this is contradicted by the fact that, in Marx's view, in the second phase of communism labour becomes a vital need. We are face to face here with a return to the ideas of the *Grundrisse*. In the *Critique of the Gotha Programme*, as in the *Grundrisse*, Marx outlines a "welfare society" in which labour becomes a vital need. There is a difference here from *Theories of Surplus Value*, where (as in *Capital*) labour appears in most instances as "social duty", something completely different from a "vital need". In the model which is outlined in *Capital* and in *Theories of Surplus Value*, production for needs is not correlated with labour as a vital need, but with labour as "social duty". The theory of the "pure dominance" of the law of value necessarily follows upon this.

Although there is no reference to it in the *Critique of the Gotha Programme*, it is probable that when Marx was writing about labour in this work, he had in mind a similar model to that in the *Grundrisse*. In fact, while it is difficult to envisage simple, unskilled mechanical labour as a "vital need", it is easy enough to envisage the skilled labour of control as a vital need: control by the human being who "appears alongside the process of production". Even more so if we bear it in mind that when Marx is talking of the reduction of labour to simple labour he never speaks of the transformation of labour into a "vital need", but stresses that labour always remains the realm of necessity, and that the realm of freedom "begins" outside it (in free time).

We shall turn now to the categories of "necessary labour", "surplus labour" and "socially necessary labour". Let us start with the *Grundrisse*.

The "labour time necessary for production" has an important role to play, especially if we bear in mind that it must diminish as far as possible and to an ever increasing degree. It cannot function as a measure, since all labour will be qualitatively different (and what is more, qualitatively different *according to the individual*) and therefore unquantifiable. The idea of reduction to "simple labour" does not appear.

"Economy of time, to this all economy ultimately reduces itself. Society likewise has to distribute its time in a purposeful way, in order to achieve a production adequate to its overall needs; . . . thus, economy of time, along with the planned distribution of labour time among the various branches of production, remains the first economic law on the basis of communal production. It becomes a law, there, to an even higher degree. However, this is essentially different from a measurement of exchange values (labour or products) by labour time. The labour of individuals in the same branch of work and the various kinds of work, are different from one another not only quantitatively but also qualitatively. What does a solely quantitative difference between things presuppose? The identity of their qualities. Hence, the quantitative measure of labours presupposes the equivalence, the identity of their quality."[101]

It is no accident that he fails to mention the reduction to "simple labour". As long as different kinds of labour are divided into simple and complex, this reduction is performed by the market. As is well known, this kind of problem does not arise in *Capital*; it is possible to measure by means of labour time with *or* without a market, because all labour is simple labour. If, however, as one finds in the *Grundrisse* and also in the *Critique of the Gotha Programme*, the labour envisaged for the future is qualitatively different not only for the various branches of industry but also for the individuals, then "the socially necessary labour time" can no longer serve as a measure. We can add a particularly striking example in relation to science: how can the socially necessary labour time be fixed in the sphere of science, how can qualitatively different types of scientific activity be compared on this basis? (In *Capital*, too, a role of prime importance in the society of associated producers is attributed to science. But in this case the "reduction to simple labour" becomes invalid, though Marx is not aware of this. In this respect the arguments in the *Grundrisse* are of greater importance.)

In the passage quoted above, material production in the future appears in Marx's view to be fully rationalised. But at the same time no criterion or measure of this rationalisation is given; its vehicle is simply the "general intellect", or the capacity for rationalisation which the society of associated producers possesses. (It is unnecessary to stress once again that the idea of labour as a vital need is inherent in this conception.)

In the *Grundrisse* there is one single concept of necessary labour, that of "socially necessary" labour. The division of the labour of an individual person into necessary and surplus labour

111

ceases at the same time as capitalism. In this case, it no longer makes sense to divide the labour time during which a man works to satisfy his "necessary needs" from the rest of his labour time, given that this latter part is likewise performed by the social individual for himself and not for the valorisation of capital. (Since every item produced directly or indirectly satisfies the needs of the socialised individual, so too, from the point of view of the individual, labour is no longer divided into necessary and surplus labour.)

"Proudhon's lack of understanding of this matter is evident from his axiom that every labour leaves a surplus. What he denies for capital he transforms into a natural property of labour. The point is, rather, that the labour time necessary to meet absolute needs leaves free time . . . and that therefore a surplus product can be created if surplus labour is worked. *The aim is to suspend the relation itself, so that the surplus product itself appears as necessary.*"[102]

One gets the impression, however, that in the *Grundrisse* Marx is already distinguishing the first phase of communism from the second, though not so explicitly as in the *Critique of the Gotha Programme*. It is absolutely clear from the latter work that in the first phase of communism it is indeed possible to make a real distinction between necessary and surplus labour. From the so-called gross yield of labour, society deducts the labour time necessary to invest in means of production, as well as the labour time which is devoted to production for the "communal satisfaction of needs" and for social purposes. The worker receives, in the form of "wages" [*Arbeitsgeld*], what he can use for the satisfaction of his personal needs; his necessary labour is also embodied in this. Man in fact works according to his capacities, but work has not yet become "vital need" for him, and true social wealth does not yet exist; and so it is *necessary* to keep necessary labour separate (however true it may be that in the last analysis all labour performed is necessary — socially necessary — labour). Whenever, in the *Grundrisse*, the notion of "wages" in the future society appears with a positive emphasis (and the emphasis is only positive when the reference is to future society), one is confronted with a prospect for the future society which Marx regarded as an immediate possibility. Marx writes that "the historic destiny (of capital) is fulfilled as soon as . . . there has been such a development of needs that surplus labour above and beyond necessity has itself become a general need arising out of individual needs themselves . . . hence where labour in which a human being does what a thing could do has ceased."[103] Here Marx "skips" the first phase of communism; but this is an exceptional case. There can be no doubt that Marx is presupposing the existence of "wages" and therefore the distinction (from the individual's point of view) between necessary and surplus labour, as well as the functioning of the law of value. Marx introduces another conception too, obviously for a more distant future: that from the point of view of the individual, there will be no distinction between necessary labour and surplus labour, and that the law of value will also have lost its function:

"As soon as labour in the direct form has ceased to be the great wellspring of wealth, labour time ceases and must cease to be its measure, and hence exchange value must cease to be the measure of use value [as we have said, the categories of value and exchange value are not differentiated here — A.H.]. . . . With that, production based on exchange value breaks down, and the direct, material production process is stripped of the form of penury and antithesis [a further example of how the contradiction is solved — A.H.]. The free development of individualities, and hence not the reduction of necessary labour time so as to posit surplus labour, but rather the general reduction of the necessary labour of society to a minimum, which then corresponds to the artistic, scientific, etc., development of the individuals in the time set free, and with the means created, for all of them."[104]

This conception, which in the *Grundrisse* and the *Critique of the Gotha Programme* characterises only the first phrase of communism, becomes dominant in Marx's exposition, once value and exchange value have been distinguished: the rationality of labour must be measured by the socially necessary labour time. The possibility is also posed, though not in such a radical and basic way, of rationally separating necessary labour from surplus labour in the society of associated producers itself. In *Theories of Surplus Value* Marx writes:

"Let us suppose however that the capital does not exist, but that the worker himself appropriates his own surplus labour, that is to say he appropriates the excess of the values that he

113

has created over the excess of the values that he has consumed. It is only of this labour that one could speak as truly productive, that is to say labour that creates new values."[105]

In the first volume of *Capital* the problem is discussed in detail. Before quoting this passage, I would like to emphasise that Marx also leaves other alternatives open, which he associates with the changeover to the communist mode of production and distribution. But from our point of view what is interesting is that he speaks before all else of a possibility of distinguishing between necessary and surplus labour:

"Let us now picture to ourselves, by way of change, a community of free individuals, carrying on their work with the means of production in common, in which the labour power of all the different individuals is consciously applied as the combined labour power of the community . . . the total product of our community is a social product. One portion serves as fresh means of production and remains social. But another portion is consumed by the members as means of subsistence. A distribution of this portion amongst them is consequently necessary. The mode of this distribution will vary with the productive organisation of community, and the degree of historical development attained by the producers. We will assume, but merely for the sake of a parallel with the production of commodities, that the share of each individual producer in the means of subsistence is determined by his labour time. Labour time would, in that case, play a double part. Its apportionment in accordance with a definite social plan maintains proper the proportion between the different kinds of work to be done and the various wants of the community. On the other hand, it also serves as a measure of the portion of the common labour borne by each individual, and of his share in the part of the total product destined for individual consumption. The social relations of the individual producers, with regard both to their labour and to its products, are in this case perfectly simple and intelligible, and that with regard not only to production but also to distribution."[106]

There can be no doubt that this conception, at least where it concerns the second function of the measure of labour time, corresponds exactly to the model which is defined in the *Critique of the Gotha Programme* as the first phase of communism, and which still bears the "birthmarks" of capitalist society.

In the second and even more in the third volume of *Capital*, there is no distinction between necessary and surplus labour as regards the individual human being, the individual producer; but the distinction is maintained with reference to the social product as a whole, i.e. with reference to the society of associated producers, considered as one huge individual. The characteristic of capitalist society is not in fact surplus labour, but its transformation into capital: "That this takes place in the shape of a transformation of profit into capital signifies merely that it is the capitalist rather than the labourer who disposes of excess labour."[107] In the same work he says: "It is only where production is under the actual, predetermining control of society that the latter establishes a relation between the volume of social labour time applied in producing definite articles, and the volume of the social want to be satisfied by these articles."[108] That is: the "associated producers" first measure the existing disposable labour time. This depends on the size of the population, and on the question of disposable hours of labour time (so much the better if this is small: the more developed the productive forces, the smaller the number of hours of labour time marked down for productive purposes). This labour time is then "subdivided" between the various branches of production, in the following way:
a) The socially necessary labour time in each branch of production is measured (rationally determined).
b) It is decided how much of this time should be used to satisfy the population's immediate needs for material goods (this is the necessary labour), and how much is available for other purposes, e.g. for the development of means of production (this is the surplus labour).

It should be stressed that this conception is clearly based upon the reduction of labour to simple labour, and therefore upon the hypothesis that the labour performed by each individual (presupposing that the level of productivity is the same) can be performed in an approximately equal time, and also that it is performed as a matter of duty. In the case of complex labour (which Marx considers in the *Grundrisse*), this kind of rationality can be introduced only by calculating separately the value of an hour's labour from each individual, which would be absurd without the existence of a market. (One may recall that it is precisely for this reason that in the *Grundrisse* measurement by means of labour time is dropped.) I repeat: measurement in terms of labour time and the distinction between necessary and surplus labour (without a market structure) is based essentially upon the whole of society being conceived as one single individual.

We still have to consider what the almost unsolvable problems are that arise here, regarding the relation between production and needs.

Without doubt Marx imagines the society of associated producers as one in which the measurement of wealth is not the proportion of necessary labour to surplus labour, but the proportion of necessary time to disposable time. It does not matter here whether Marx does or does not differentiate between necessary and surplus labour. Naturally the development of productive forces is a precondition for the increase in disposable time; but true wealth for human beings is realised in the free types of self-activity in disposable time.

The idea is, in itself, clear and non-contradictory. The problems only arise when we examine the relation between *disposable time* and *production or consumption*.

"Disposable time" is time for consumption, not for labour; it is time, on the one hand, for enjoyment derived from the use of material goods, and on the other hand for free intellectual activities which, to the extent that they require ready-produced means, belong likewise to the sphere of consumption (which could also be called "creative consumption"). We are not taking into consideration here those purely intellectual needs which are satisfied during disposable time.

The problem arises of whether those activities which Marx places in the category of consumption, but which are indispensable conditions and moments of production, are performed in "necessary" or in "disposable" time. For example, the "social satisfaction of needs" (e.g. training) and the control of production belong to this group.

It *seems* natural that they should be performed during "necessary time". The conception set out in the *Grundrisse* is consistently in line with this interpretation. Since labour of the old type no longer exists, production is controlled by a qualitatively different type of activity; and since the necessary labour is not measured in labour time, *every* type of activity playing a role in production is a constituent part of this necessary time. If, however, we look at the third volume of *Capital*, we shall find that the answer is not so easy. According to the conception outlined there, necessary time consists in the performance of *simple* labour.

For Marx, training and the control of production cannot be considered as simple labour, and so they cannot belong to the system of "exchange" of simple labour. One may of course suppose that individuals perform the tasks of control and direction over and above their necessary labour, and that their "free self-activity" lies in precisely this. If this were so, however, it would mean that one particular socially necessary labour would be an organic part of "disposable time" and could not be included in "socially necessary labour time". We can certainly imagine the exchange of labours within necessary time; however, it would not be an exchange between simple kinds of labour, but between simple and complex labour. And where do people develop the capacities which qualify them for the work of control? If we reply "in necessary time", then the theory of "simple labour" collapses completely, for in the process of "exchanging" labours, everyone — for the time being — is doing the controlling, and everyone has to master the performance of complex labour processes: in this way, the proportion of necessary time allocated for actual productive labour would be extraordinarily reduced. If this mastery of complex labour processes is developed during disposable time, we are back again with our previous contradiction. In fact, it makes no difference one way or the other whether, during their free time, people perform simple labour or train themselves for complex labour: in either event, a part of their free time is "socially necessary" and is not measurable in "socially necessary labour time".

The problem becomes even more striking if we consider the function of the natural sciences. Natural science, in Marx's view, is the greatest productive force; scientific labour is "labour in general". If the performance of scientific labour and the training needed for it belong to necessary time (as it obviously should) then specialisation ensues; this contradicts the conception presented in *Capital*, not only in the sense that different people specialise in different branches of science, but also in the sense that *certain* people specialise in the natural sciences in general (these people perform complex labour, the others simple labour). A kind of specialisation in which *everyone* masters a particular branch of the natural sciences and practises it alternately with simple labour, would likewise drastically reduce the time assigned to direct production. If, instead, training in a branch of the natural sciences belongs to the sphere of free activities during disposable time, then once again this cannot be measured by socially necessary labour time. (Personally I can imagine, in the far distant future, a model in which "everyone is an expert in some field", but only with the aid of an allocation of disposable time, and only with a completely different determination of value from that which is presented in the third volume of *Capital*.)

Now we can discuss the interaction between production and the structure of needs in the society of associated producers.

We have already noted that in his conception of the society of associated producers, Marx is working with an altogether new structure of needs. The primary role here is played by the need for labour (by which the whole theory stands or falls) and, as we have seen, by the need for surplus labour.

We know that the origin of the need for labour and its growth into a "vital need" are not synonymous for Marx. In capitalism labour is a burden, (a) because it is performed under external compulsion, because it is alienated, and (b) because its specific nature offers no possibility of self-realisation:

"He (Adam Smith) is right, of course, that, in its historic forms as slave labour, serf-labour, and wage-labour, labour always appears as repulsive, always as external forced labour; and not-labour, by contrast, as 'freedom and happiness'. This holds doubly: for this contradictory labour; and, relatedly, for labour which has not yet created the subjective and objective conditions for itself . . . in which labour becomes attractive work, the individual's self-realisation, which in no way means that it becomes mere fun, mere amusement, as Fourier, with Grisette-like naiveté, conceives it."[109]

Marx uses the composition of music as an example of the kind of labour that is purely intellectual.

In the *Grundrisse* both conditions are satisfied: alienation is overcome and labour becomes *travail attractif*. Since with the production of material goods labour in the traditional sense ceases, all labour becomes essentially intellectual labour, the field for the self-realisation of the human personality. It thus becomes the vital need, a determining (even if not the most determining) human need, and hence it also assumes a dominant role in the structure of needs. In this conception, there never can arise any question about "why" human beings work.

In the framework of *Capital*, however, only one condition is satisfied: the alienation of labour ceases (in every aspect), but labour itself does not become *travail attractif*. In this interpretation labour in the society of associated producers is not free self-activity:

"In fact, the realm of freedom actually begins only where labour which is determined by necessity and mundane considerations cease; thus in the very nature of things it lies beyond the sphere of actual material production. . . . freedom in this field can only consist in socialised man, the associated producers, rationally regulating their interchange with nature, bringing it under their common control, instead of being ruled by it as by the blind forces of nature; and achieving this with the least expenditure of energy and under conditions most favourable to, and worthy of, their human nature. But it nonetheless still remains a realm of necessity. Beyond it begins that development of human energy which is an end in itself, the true realm of freedom, which, however, can blossom forth only with this realm of necessity as its basis. The shortening of the working day is its basic pre-requisite."[110]

Three comments need to be made here. First, since according to the quotation from *Capital* only free time is the sphere of free self-activity, Marx is attributing an even greater importance here than in the *Grundrisse* to time-economy, to the reduction of the necessary working time and to the rationalisation of production. Secondly, since labour is not itself *travail attractif*, it may be asked why people work. Thirdly, I would like to emphasise that from this point of view the project here appears just as utopian, despite the fact that its presentation is more realistic, as in the *Grundrisse*; I believe it inconceivable that there should be such a huge abyss between the activity of labour and the activity of free time. The *Grundrisse*'s noble picture of the individual active in

119

his free time who re-enters production a changed man would lose its relevance: production does not "need" to be performed by "changed", "richer" human beings.

This discussion could take us far away from our real argument, so let us return to the second question: why do people work? Assuming the structure of needs to be what it is today, the answer can only be conceived in terms of the general obligation to labour. But "the obligation to labour" for Marx is characteristic only of a period of transition (the brief phase of the dictatorship of the proletariat). In the society of associated producers only nature can force people to do anything: no one can force anyone else (feudal lordship and serfdom are, in Marx's view, reciprocal determinations; there is no feudal lordship without serfdom and vice versa). In the first phase of communism (in which people share products according to their labour) there is naturally a form of obligation inherited from capitalism: in order to live, people must work. But when they share their goods according to their needs, and the labour time of each individual is not divided into necessary labour and surplus labour, then this form of obligation also ceases to exist. So why do human beings work? In *Capital*, Marx posits a structure of needs that is basically new, that transforms human beings into changed people, for whom "social duty" is *not only an external but an internal motivation*: in this respect, "Must" [*Müssen*] and "Ought" [*Sollen*] now coincide. (I can only imagine this model in a society composed of communities. We shall see below how this hypothesis occurred to Marx.)

Only in *Capital* do we find a consistent conception of the interaction between material needs and production:

"It is only where production is under the actual, predetermining control of society that the latter establishes a relation between the volume of social labour time applied in producing definite articles, and the volume of the social want to be satisfied by these articles."[11]

And further on:

"Secondly, after the abolition of the capitalist mode of production, but still retaining social production, the determination of value continues to prevail in the sense that the regulation of labour-time and the distribution of social labour among the various production groups, ultimately the book-keeping

120

encompassing all this, become more essential than ever."[112]
And again:

"Surplus labour in general as labour performed over and above
the given requirements, must always remain. . . . a definite
quantity of surplus labour is required as insurance against
accidents, and by the necessary and progressive expansion of
the process of reproduction in keeping with the development
of the needs and the growth of population, which is called
accumulation from the viewpoint of the capitalist."[113]

What then, according to this point of view, is the relationship
between material needs and production?

Society produces *for* needs; hence the "accidental" character
of the market is eliminated. It is therefore possible, according to
Marx, to avoid the "waste" of material goods and productive
capacities which characterises capitalism and stems from the fact
that production and needs are brought together only on the
market. How are needs and production matched? The "associated
producers", as I have already indicated, will measure (a) needs
and (b) their disposable labour time, and will fix (c) the labour
time socially necessary for each activity. They will then divide up
(and re-allocate) the productive forces between various branches
of production. They will, of course, also take into account the
production that does not directly serve the satisfaction of needs
(the expansion of production, insurance funds and — they are
not mentioned here, but they appear in other passages — public
investments that will satisfy needs only over a period of time).

What are the needs which must be measured and for which
production must be undertaken? They are the "true social needs"
which are identified with "necessary needs".

But how can "true social needs" be measured? It is assumed
that the needs of individuals that are directly oriented towards
consumption are, both qualitatively and quantitatively, roughly
equal. It is therefore extraordinarily easy to account for them:
with the aid of random samples, both quality and quantity can
be determined. So far so good: but human beings in communist
society, in Marx's view, are characterised above all else by the
fact that their needs, considered *individually*, and the needs of
different individuals, will be qualitatively and quantitatively
extremely varied. If this is also true of material needs, the kind of
measurement given in *Capital* is simply absurd. Even if a pro-

121

cedure were invented — it would be indeed a complex one — to carry it out, one could assert with some certainty that such a "production for needs" would lead to a "waste" of material goods and productive forces much greater than that to which the production of commodities (regulation by the market) has led or can lead. We would thus be saying that Marx did not apply the individualisation of needs to the field of need for material goods. Only non-quantifiable types of need would become individual (and qualitatively different); quantifiable types of need (true material needs) would not become individual. This would lead to an extremely homogeneous and almost uniform image of the individual — if, that is, one accepts that Marx regarded material needs as playing a decisive role in the structure of needs of individuals. But Marx actually thought exactly the opposite: that for individuals in the society of associated producers, material needs occupy a subordinate role in the structure of needs, so that the development of a system of individual needs becomes possible notwithstanding their qualitative and quantitative "equality".

This conception is based upon relatively static needs which develop very slowly (at least where material needs are concerned). It does not even take into consideration the fact that, as we have said, purely qualitative needs (which are *eo ipso* individual) also call for material production, and that this raises further difficulties in "calculating" them.

In this conception of material needs, a kind of "egalitarianism" predominates. It is important to underline this point because "egalitarianism" has no bitterer enemy than Marx himself. He holds that the concept of equality belongs to commodity production: in fact commodity production is "realised equality". Equality and inequality are reciprocally determined: where there is equality there is inequality, and vice versa. "Equality" as a slogan and as a demand always remains within the horizon of bourgeois society. It abstracts from the uniqueness of the individual, and quantifies what is qualitatively diverse. In the society that develops the wealth of individuality — in communist society — "equality" is not realised: equality and inequality as reciprocal determinations become meaningless and irrelevant. In order to demonstrate that this idea is constantly present in Marx's thought I shall cite two passages: one from a work of his youth, the other from a late work. In *The Holy Family* Marx writes:

"Proudhon did not succeed in giving this thought the appropriate development. The idea of 'equal possession' is a political-economic one and therefore itself still an *alienated* expression for the principle that the object as being for man, as the objectified being of man, is at the same time the existence of man for other men, his human relation to other men, the social relation of man to man."[114]

The idea of "equal possession" therefore articulates, in an alienated manner (i.e. within the horizon of bourgeois society and with its terminology), the real aim, which is to overcome the alienated relations. In the *Critique of the Gotha Programme* Marx does not attack the concept of equal possession but that of equal right (equal right, as we know, will continue to subsist in the first phase of communism, which therefore will still be a bourgeois society in this respect): "This equal right . . . is therefore a right to inequality in its content, like every right."[115] This equality is "abstraction", because it takes account of man only as worker. At the same time it abstracts from the effective needs of individuals, by furnishing them with equal amounts of goods from the social wealth according equal amounts of labour, whatever their needs actually are. Distribution according to needs, in contrast to distribution according to labour, overcomes both this equality and this inequality.

According to the *Critique of the Gotha Programme*, as we know, *no value* exists in the second phase of communism, and labour is not reduced to simple labour; at the same time Marx posits an extraordinary wealth of goods. Precisely for this reason there is no place for what we have called the "egalitarian" aspect of communism. This is not the case in *Capital*, where we come across a "saturation model" regarding material goods. In Marx's conception, this kind of "egalitarianism" is in no way identical with the equality of commodity production (equality of possession and of rights): the matter at issue is rather the relative equality of actual needs as regards material goods. These, as we know, are only limited by other (higher) needs of individuals. We ourselves cannot imagine any social order in which the need for material goods can become saturated relatively easily and where the individuality of needs develops exclusively through non-material needs. Today, we would call the conception which appears in *Capital* "egalitarian". However, the fact is that it was not an egalitarian one in Marx's eyes, and that he associated this model not with "equality" but with the complete restructuring of the system of needs.

The great importance that Marx attached to the restructuring of the system of needs also appears clearly in two observations in the *Grundrisse* (in his maturity Marx considered such a restructuring to be a *sine qua non*; on this point there is no difference between *Capital* and the *Grundrisse*). He writes about workers in capitalism as follows:

"Through excessive exhaustion of their powers, brought about by lengthy, drawn-out monotonous occupations, they are seduced into habits of intemperance, and made unfit for thinking or reflection. They can have no physical, intellectual or moral 'amusements' other than of the worst sort."[116]

The intemperance follows from the fact that no capacity for physical, intellectual and moral "amusements" can develop in the worker. In the "society of associated producers", in which this capacity (qualitative needs) is well developed, "intemperance" ceases. In another passage Marx expounds the problem with reference to the social whole. If society has attained a certain level of (material) wealth, then "society (is) able to wait; . . . a large part of the wealth already created can be withdrawn both from immediate consumption and from production for immediate consumption".[117] Let me repeat once again: for material needs, Marx is using something quite close to a "saturation model", at least when he analyses the period after the attainment of a certain level of material wealth.

At this point the following question arises: who makes the decisions about how productive capacity should be allocated? Who decides, for example, how long the production of goods directly serving consumption can "wait"? Marx's reply, of course, is *everyone* (this is precisely why he speaks of "associated individuals"). But how can every individual make such decisions? Marx did not answer this question, because for him it did not arise. For us, however, in our times, it has become perhaps the most decisive question of all. The focal point of contemporary marxism is to work out models for this (or at least it ought to be).

Naturally, it is no accident that Marx did not even once formulate the question about "how every individual can take part in decision-making". We have already noted that in his opinion the category of interest will be irrelevant in the society of the future, and that there will therefore be no group interests, nor conflict of interests. The clear common interest of every member of society, apart from the satisfaction of necessary needs (which, as we have seen, still play a subordinate role in the structure of needs), will be the reduction of labour time. This is possible only through the maximum of rationalisation. Consequently, every individual strives for the same thing, namely this maximum of rationalism; and the manner in which decision-making is carried on is of no consequence whatever. Whether the decisions are made by means of a referendum or through rotating representatives, every individual expresses the needs of all other individuals and it cannot be otherwise. In "socialised" man, the human species and the individual represent a realised unity. Every individual represents the species and the species is represented in every individual. The needs of "socialised" human beings determine production — and this means that the human species itself makes the decisions.

To put it in hegelian terms, in Marx's society of associated producers the sphere of "the objective spirit" goes up in smoke. We find no system of right, no institutions or politics there. What remains of the sphere of the "objective spirit" of class society is elevated to the sphere of the "absolute spirit". For it is not only the pre-existing activities and objectivations (in an alienated form) of class society, such as art or philosophy, which are "in conformity with the species for itself". Morals too, and every human relationship, become "in conformity with the species for itself". To continue with the hegelian analogy: the "world spirit" is not only recognised in art and philosophy, but in every human relationship; every individual is representative of a conformity to the species that has become real and actual, he recognises this representativeness in every other person, and presents himself as such in relation to them. All this is very well expressed in *The Holy Family*, where Marx speaks of morality in the future:
"Plato admitted that the law must be one-sided and must make abstraction of the individual. On the other hand, under human conditions punishment will really be nothing but the sentence passed by the culprit on himself. There will be no attempt to persuade him that violence from without, exerted by others, is violence exerted on himself by himself. On the

125

contrary, he will see in other people his natural saviours from the sentence which he has pronounced on himself; in other words the relation will be reversed."[118]

In one of Kant's hypotheses he imagined "the ideal society" to be that in which people make a contract to proceed according to the categoric imperative. From the point of view of his own philosophy this is in effect a contradiction: if it is a case of making a contract, morality is changed into legality. In Marx's eyes, the same model — at least from the philosophical standpoint — appears to be posed without any contradiction. If every individual represents conformity with the species for itself, then the *need* of every individual (in this case, moral need) is involved at the level of this conformity. If his own particularity transgresses this conformity, he may therefore punish himself. The conflict between morality and legality is thus surmounted, since the opposition or opposed Being between morality and legality (which for Marx is found only in class society, in alienation) disappears.

The disappearance of legality and of all institutions does not of course imply the simple disappearance of objectivation. Quite the opposite. Only in communism (in the positive abolition of private property) is individual possession properly founded. Remember: needs are always directed towards objects. These objectivations are all "for themselves" — except the sphere of production, which is in and for itself. Since we can no longer speak of material needs, but only of needs which "stand outside them", every objectivation belongs to the realm of the "absolute spirit". Non-material needs are therefore all directed to the "absolute spirit", to their objectivations, to their objects and to the allocation of these objects.

It is precisely for this reason that in the society of associated producers the need for "free time", for "leisure time", has such a leading role in man's system of needs. ("Leisure time" is not necessarily synonymous with "free time": the latter can in fact be interpreted as a negative concept, as freedom from labour. For Marx, however, free time is "leisure time", an unambiguously positive category: time for genuinely human, high-level activities — free activities.) Furthermore, artistic activity has a leading role in free-time activities, as the work of Marx's most creative periods clearly demonstrates. Artistic activity, which even in the era of class society is already drawn towards objectivations "for themselves" and creates them, is the simplest and most illuminating example of what preoccupies Marx: the need for objectivations which are objectivations *for themselves* and which conform to the species, is the true human need of the members of the "society of associated producers".

Needs for objectivations (and objects) for themselves are purely qualitative needs, which are not quantifiable; furthermore, they are always needs to an end. This is formulated in the third volume of *Capital* as follows: beyond production "begins that *development of human energy* which is an *end in itself*, the true *realm of freedom*."[119] In activities which are directed towards objectivations for themselves, the true wealth of human beings develops, a universality of needs and capacities that satisfies qualitatively different (non-quantifiable) needs: "Wealth is disposable time and nothing more."[120]

The object for itself of needs can, as we have already noted, be not only an objectivation but also the other person. Recall the *Economic and Philosophic Manuscripts of 1844*: in his human relationships, socialised man at all times makes qualities possible only for other men, and this is an end in itself; "rich man" is man rich in human relationships. The question here is: does need for human beings also mean "need for community"?

The question is of significance not only for the system of needs, but also for the whole social model. We have seen that in Marx's notion of the society of associated producers there is no place for the "objective spirit", for the system of institutions. But should this also imply that there is no place for human integration?

For Marx, community (even on the smallest scale) is justifiable and relevant only when it appears as the immediate form of conformity to the species for itself, when it is an objectivation that conforms with the species for itself. There is no interest, and no conflict of interests: community, like the individual, can only be an *immediate* expression of such conformity to the species.

In the young Marx, community and the need for community undoubtedly appear as a leitmotiv. Remember his thoughts on the meetings of communist workers: "But at the same time, as a result of this association, they acquire a new need — the need for society — and what appears as a means becomes an end."[121] In the same work he also says: "Although communal activity and communal enjoyment — i.e. activity and enjoyment which are manifested and directly revealed in real association with other men — will occur wherever such a direct expression of sociability stems from the true character of the activity's content and is adequate to its nature."[122] Or again: "In the same way, the senses and enjoyment of other men have become my own appropriation. Besides these direct organs, therefore, social organs develop in the form of society; thus, for instance, activity in direct association with others, etc., has become an organ for expressing my own life, and a mode of appropriating human life."[123] "Universal consciousness", reflection, philosophy, theory and thought must be rooted in this communal Being, and not "grip the masses" merely after the event. "My general consciousness is only the theoretical shape of that which the living shape is the real community, the social fabric, although at the present time general consciousness is an abstraction from real life and as such confronts it with hostility."[124] This is why I stated earlier that, in Marx's view, not all philosophy will cease under communism, but only the philosophy which counterposes the particular to that which conforms with the species, and which counterposes appearance to essence — the philosophy built on self-realising values. It is social science instead which, according to this conception, would seem to cease. In fact there will no longer be any fetishism; in society essence and appearance will overlap. And so social science, which owes its existence to the contradiction between essence and appearance, will in effect be superfluous under communism according to Marx's view.

The idea of community and of the need for society, which is properly central in the works of his youth, moves somewhat into the background in his later works. We can see various reasons for this. First, there is his critique of the "community" of natural societies and its "limitedness". Wherever Marx speaks of community — even in his earlier works — he is thinking of something different from "natural communities". He conceives the communities of the future as freely chosen, as made up of individuals who freely unite, as "purely social" relations — a consequence of the pushing back of natural limits. However, as Marx devotes himself with increasing intensity to his analysis of the evolution of capitalism as alienated *evolution*, he puts increasing emphasis on the positive trend which capitalism has produced — amongst other things, by dissolving the natural communities. But there is another factor to be taken into account: that the presence of communities in the future society seemed so obvious to Marx that he did not see any necessity for discussing it separately. Very often he speaks of the society of the future as the "society of co-operatives"! The existence of the "community" and the "need for community" in effect pass into the background; and in the few passages where he speaks of them, they appear as a "natural" perspective. This is how he deals with it in the third volume of *Capital*, for example. Analysing the embryos of the future which exist in the present, he speaks of Robert Owen's co-operative factories:

"The co-operative factories of the labourers themselves represent, *within the old form, the first shoots of the new* . . . the capitalist stock companies, as much as the co-operative factories, should be considered as *transitional forms* from the capitalist mode of production to the associated one, with the only distinction that *the antagonism is resolved negatively in the one and positively in the other*."[125]

In the draft of a letter to Vera Zasulic, written in 1881, Marx expresses himself in a still more broad and unambiguous manner. The Russian rural community "finds capitalism in a crisis that will end only with its elimination, and *with the return of the modern societies* to the 'archaic' type of communal property; or, as an American author has said, the new system to which modern society is tending will be a revival in a superior form of an archaic social type. There is no need to be frightened of the expression 'archaic'." Furthermore, in discussing those aspects of the communities of the future which will be different from the archaic communities, he points before all else to the fact that the former will not be based upon blood ties. This conception is in no way different from the position taken by Engels in his article of 1845, "Description of the communist colonies that have originated in recent times and are still existing", in which he refers enthusiastically to the religious communes of the United States and predicts that they will spread. Marx was alarmed by the dissolution of the existing communities, because he recognised and treasured them as embryos of the form of intercourse and integration which in communism would become general.

In Marx's view, therefore, the "everyday life" of man in the

129

future society is not built around productive labour. On the contrary, productive labour occupies a subordinate position in the activities of everyday life; the centre of organisation of life is represented by those activities and human relationships which conform with the species for itself. The needs directed towards these (qualitative needs-as-ends) will become man's primary needs, they will constitute his unique individuality and will limit needs for material goods. It is in this way that the personality that is "deep" and rich in needs will be constituted.

Marx believed this change in the structure of needs to be "natural" and "obvious". He took so little account of the possibility of conflicts that one thing must be repeated: although the change in Being is the decisive issue for him, there are quite a few Enlightenment aspects to be found in his conception. One will search in vain for the actual conflicts and problems of the transition which are so relevant for us and which are now a century old, but even so this "pure" model has not lost its decisive significance for us.

Engels spoke with pride of the development of socialism from utopia to science. Today, science contains more than a few utopian elements. But as Ernst Bloch has so strikingly said, there are fertile and infertile utopias. There are many respects in which Marx's ideas on the society of associated producers and on the system of needs of united individuals are utopian, when measured against our own today and our own possibilities for action; they are nonetheless *fertile*. He establishes a norm against which we can measure the reality and value of our ideas, and with which we can determine the limitedness of our actions: it expresses the most beautiful aspiration of mature humanity, an aspiration that belongs to our Being.

NOTES

1   Marx, *Capital* (Moscow: Foreign Languages Publishing House, 1961), Vol. I, p.35.
2   Ibid., Vol. I, p. 620-1.
3   Marx, *Economic and Philosophic Manuscripts of 1844* (London: Lawrence and Wishart, 1970), p. 149-50.
4   Ibid., p. 159.
5   Ibid., p. 113.
6   Marx, *Grundrisse* (London: Penguin Books, 1973), p. 92.
7   Ibid., p. 325.
8   Ibid., p. 528.
9   *Capital*, Vol. I, p. 171. Translation modified.
10 Ibid., p. 519.
11 Ibid., p. 559.
12 *Capital*, Vol. III, p. 799-800.
13 Ibid., p. 800. Translation modified.
14 Marx, *The Poverty of Philosophy* (London: Lawrence and Wishart, 1970), p. 68.
15 *Capital*, Vol. II, p. 403.
16 Ibid., p. 410.
17 *Economic and Philosophic Manuscripts of 1844*, p. 143-4.
18 Ibid., p. 147.
19 *Capital*, Vol. III, p. 252.
20 Marx, *The German Ideology* (London: Lawrence and Wishart, 1965), p. 87.
21 *Economic and Philosophic Manuscripts of 1844*, p. 141.
22 *The German Ideology*, p. 39.
23 Ibid., p. 276.
24 Ibid., p. 277.
25 Ibid., p. 277.
26 Ibid., p. 459.
27 *Economic and Philosophic Manuscripts of 1844*, p. 182. Translation modified.
28 *Grundrisse*, p. 409.
29 *Capital*, Vol. I, p. 432.
30 *Economic and Philosophic Manuscripts of 1844*, p. 137. Translation modified.
31 *Grundrisse*, p. 84.
32 *Economic and Philosophic Manuscripts of 1844*, p. 155.
33 Ibid., p. 155.
34 Ibid., p. 147. Translation modified.
35 Ibid., p. 147.

36   Ibid., p. 168.
37   *Grundrisse*, p. 222.
38   Ibid., p. 224.
39   Ibid., p. 415-16.
40   Ibid. Marx is quoting, in Latin, from the Book of Revelation.
41   *Economic and Philosophic Manuscripts of 1844*, p. 167.
42   Ibid., p. 169. Translation modified.
43   *Grundrisse*, p. 224.
44   *Economic and Philosophic Manuscripts of 1844*, p. 139.
45   Ibid., p. 150.
46   Ibid., p. 151.
47   *Grundrisse*, p. 422.
48   *Economic and Philosophic Manuscripts of 1844*, p. 139.
49   Ibid., p. 139.
50   Marx and Engels, *The Holy Family* (London: Lawrence and Wishart, 1956), p. 152-3.
51   Ibid., p. 163.
52   Ibid., p. 165.
53   Ibid., p. 267.
54   *Grundrisse*, p. 244.
55   Marx, "Wage Labour and Capital", in *Selected Works* (Moscow, 1935), Vol. I, pp. 268 and 273.
56   Marx, "Value, Price and Profit", Ibid., p. 337.
57   *Capital*, Vol. III, p. 253.
58   Ibid., p. 178. Translation modified.
59   Ibid., p. 185. Translation modified.
60   *Selected Works*, Vol. II, p. 562.
61   Ibid., p. 562.
62   *Capital*, Vol. I, p. 10.
63   Marx, *Theories of Surplus Value* (London: Lawrence and Wishart, 1972), Vol. III, p. 429.
64   *Capital*, Vol. I, p. 620-1.
65   Ibid., p. 10.
66   Letter to the editors of *Otecestvennye Zapiski*.
67   *The Poverty of Philosophy*, p. 123-4.
68   *Grundrisse*, p. 99.
69   Ibid., p. 706.
70   Marx, *A Contribution to the Critique of Political Economy* (London: Lawrence and Wishart, 1971), p. 153.
71   *Capital*, Vol. I, p. 763. Translation modified.
72   Ibid., p. 763.
73   Engels, *Anti-Dühring* (London: Lawrence and Wishart, 1955), p. 388.

74 *Capital*, Vol. I, p. 75.
75 Ibid., p. 81, footnote 2.
76 Ibid., p. 81.
77 *Capital*, Vol. III, p. 256.
78 *Theories of Surplus Value*, Vol. II, p. 118.
79 *The Poverty of Philosophy*, p. 197.
80 See *Critique of Hegel's Philosophy of Right* (Cambridge: Cambridge University Press, 1970), p. 137.
81 Ibid., p. 138. Translation modified.
82 *The German Ideology*, p. 93.
93 Ibid., p. 94.
84 *Capital*, Vol. I. Translation modified.
85 *The German Ideology*, p. 483.
86 *The Poverty of Philosophy*, p. 161.
87 *Capital*, Vol. I, p. 487-8. Translation modified.
88 Ibid., p. 490. Translation modified.
89 *Grundrisse*, p. 463. Translation modified.
90 Ibid., p. 461.
91 *The Poverty of Philosophy*, p. 45.
92 *Grundrisse*, p. 712.
93 Ibid., p. 527-8.
94 Marx and Engels, "The Manifesto of the Communist Party", in *Selected Works*, Vol. I, p. 227.
95 *Theories of Surplus Value*, Vol. III, p. 267. Translation modified.
96 *Grundrisse*, p. 705.
97 *Theories of Surplus Value*, Vol. III, p. 257.
98 Ibid., p. 273. Translation modified.
99 Ibid., p. 276 (footnote).
100 Marx, "Critique of the Gotha Programme", in *Selected Works*, Vol. II, p. 563. Translation modified.
101 *Grundrisse*, p. 173.
102 Ibid., p. 612.
103 Ibid., p. 325.
104 Ibid., p. 705-6.
105 *Theories of Surplus Value*, Vol. I, p. 253.
106 *Capital*, Vol. I, p. 78-9.
107 Ibid., Vol. III, p. 828.
108 Ibid., p. 184.
109 *Grundrisse*, p. 611.
110 *Capital*, Vol. III, p. 799-800.
111 Ibid., p. 184.
112 Ibid., p. 830.
113 Ibid., p. 799.

114   *The Holy Family*, p. 60.
115   "Critique of the Gotha Programme", in *Selected Works*, Vol. II, p. 564.
116   *Grundrisse*, p. 714. Marx is actually quoting Robert Owen.
117   Ibid., p. 707.
118   *The Holy Family*, p. 238-9.
119   *Capital*, Vol. III, p. 800.
120   *Theories of Surplus Value*, Vol. III, p. 255.
121   *Economic and Philosophic Manuscripts of 1844*, p. 137.
122   Ibid., p. 137. Translation modified.
123   Ibid., p. 139-40. Translation modified.
124   Ibid., p. 137.
125   *Capital*, Vol. III, p. 431.